DI016922

Case Studies in Sport Psychology

The Jones and Bartlett Series in Health and Physical Education

NATIONAL UNIVERSITY
LIBRARY   SAN DIEGO

CASE STUDIES IN SPORT PSYCHOLOGY

Bob Rotella, PhD
University of Virginia, Charlottesville, Virginia

B. Ann Boyce, PhD
University of Virginia, Charlottesville, Virginia

Bill Allyson, PhD
Macalester College, Saint Paul, Minnesota

Jacqueline C. Savis, PhD
Pacific Lutheran University, Tacoma, Washington

JONES AND BARTLETT PUBLISHERS
Sudbury, Massachusetts
BOSTON   LONDON   SINGAPORE

NATIONAL UNIVERSITY
LIBRARY
SAN DIEGO

Editorial, Sales, and Customer Service Offices
Jones and Bartlett Publishers
40 Tall Pine Drive
Sudbury, MA 01776
(508) 443-5000
info@jbpub.com
http://www.jbpub.com

Jones and Bartlett Publishers International
Barb House, Barb Mews
London W6 7PA
UK

Copyright © 1998 by Jones and Bartlett Publishers, Inc.
All rights reserved. No part of the material protected by this copyright notice may be reproduced or utilized in any form, electronic or mechanical, including photocopying, recording, or by any information storage and retrieval system, without written permission by the copyright owner.

Library of Congress Cataloging-in-Publication Data
Case studies in sport psychology / Bob Rotella . . . [et al.].
p. cm.
Includes bibliographical references.
ISBN 0-7637-0355-9
1. Sports—Psychological aspects—Case Studies. 2. Athletes—Psychology—Case studies. I. Rotella, Robert J.
GV706.4.C37 1998
796'.01—dc21 97-9654
CIP

Vice President and Acquisitions Editor: Joseph E. Burns
Production Editor: Martha Stearns
Manufacturing Buyer: Jenna Sturgis
Design: Steve Dyer
Editorial Production Service: Joan M. Flaherty
Typesetting: UltraGraphics
Cover Design: Hannus Design Associates
Printing and Binding: Malloy Lithographing

Printed in the United States of America
02 01 00 99 98 10 9 8 7 6 5 4 3 2 1

Contents

Preface

THIS BOOK WAS WRITTEN for a variety of reasons. First and foremost, my experience in preparing graduate students at The University of Virginia has convinced me of the importance of case studies for proficiency in applied sport psychology consulting. Students must study and thoroughly understand theory and research, and be well-educated in mental training strategies. Then, by applying their abilities and knowledge as they work through case studies, students move beyond giving canned responses and learn to provide real-life solutions.

A second reason for writing this case studies book is my belief that it takes practice and experience to become an effective and efficient consultant. Creative thinking, problem solving, and the ability to think on one's feet in response to uncertain and unpredictable situations is essential. By working through these cases, students will gain experience in the classroom, where mistakes can be freely discussed, corrected, and learned from without real-life consequences.

Finally, in working through cases, students have the opportunity to develop a solid philosophy and their own methods. As they listen to and work through different cases, they soon learn that although there are no right or wrong solutions, there *are* solutions that are logically thought out, theory based, and explainable and defensible.

During my 20 years at the university, an array of cases have proved to be effective. This book shares these cases with faculty members, students, and applied sport consultants around the world. It is my hope that this resource will play a helpful role in raising the quality of graduate training in sport psychology and the quality of help given to athletes and coaches.

Repeated experiences with a variety of cases involving different levels of sport competition, different sports, and various age groups can play an important role in ensuring the continued growth and success of applied sport psychology consultation. It is my hope that this book will be only the beginning of the use of the case-study method for training future consultants. I also hope that the case-studies approach will lead to a greater appreciation of the importance of problem-solving skills as the field we all love so much continues to evolve.

I wish to thank my good friend and colleague Dr. Ann Boyce for her help in my evolution and understanding of the case-studies method, and for her assistance in organizing this book. I also wish to thank Dr. Bill Allyson for his countless hours of overseeing every phase of the project, and Dr. Jackie Savis for her work with me and the graduate students in selecting the best submissions and helping rewrite and edit cases.

Dr. Bob Rotella

Introduction

THE FORMAL USE OF CASES is a relatively new phenomenon in the training of sport psychology consultants, although it has been a standard teaching methodology in business, medicine, and law for many years. Based on real-life events, cases are problem-centered stories that culminate in a dilemma. The value of the case-study teaching approach is in the analysis of the problem, the generation of potential solutions, and the evaluation of those solutions in light of feasibility, current theory, and ramifications.

The case-study teaching approach is an exciting as well as challenging way to prepare sport psychology consultants. Case studies represent a departure from the traditional lecture style wherein instructors provide information and give ready-made answers to students' questions. The case-study approach challenges students not only to understand theory, but also to apply it in practical situations. Case studies demand thoughtful consideration as well as action-oriented solutions to real-world dilemmas. In addition, class discussions provide a safe haven in which students can develop and enhance their skills as future consultants without putting their jobs at risk.

The cases in this book, which focus on pertinent issues in sport psychology, were written specifically to enhance the development of future sport psychology consultants. They originate from the experiences of practitioners, instructors, and graduate students of sport psychology and performance enhancement. The need for case-study practice is most apparent in the development of sound young professionals upon whom the future of this profession rests. The cases are also valuable for advanced practitioners and instructors who wish to gain competence in areas they have not yet experienced with athletes.

We have attempted to provide a wide range of experiential cases for students to think through. There is no single right answer to any case. Learning takes place in the process of contemplating the issues, posing and answering relevant questions, discussing alternatives, and applying strategies.

The practice of sport psychology requires daily, if not hourly, problem analysis and decision making. We hope that experiences with cases will help future consultants develop problem-solving skills and become reflective and critical about their abilities. We also hope that the cases in this book serve as the catalyst for many heated and thoughtful discussions.

Organization of the Book

Case Studies in Sport Psychology is designed as a supplement for sport psychology textbooks, providing material for classroom discussions. Each case in this book presents a unique dilemma. Based on their dominant themes, the cases are organized into 15 chapters, which together address the specific issues and theories covered in most sport psychology classes. It is assumed that the instructor will select cases that match the issues and theories currently being studied. As readers will notice, some cases touch on more than one theme; thus there may be some overlap among chapters.

To the Instructor

The role of the instructor in the case-study process is that of group facilitator. When you use the case-study approach, you must refrain from offering solutions or advice. The goal of this approach is to give future consultants practical experience in problem solving so they can develop the skills they will need to be successful.

At the end of each case is a set of questions that will stimulate the students' thinking about relevant issues and strategies. These questions address key points from each case and provide a framework for facilitating class discussion, but they are not intended to be complete guidelines for analysis. Feel free to revise the questions as the class discussion evolves. It is likely that the class will discover additional issues (e.g., pertinent strategies or theories) not prompted by the questions. This is expected and is part of the process of working with these cases. In the appendix, "Teaching Suggestions," you will find advice for using the question guides provided and for creating new ones.

Also at the end of the book is a list of suggested references for each chapter's topic. This list directs students to a limited amount of theory and application that may help them work through the cases. The suggested references do not cover all possible sources of theory or application; you can provide additional reference lists to direct students to other useful materials. The teaching suggestions in the appendix also provide alternatives for your use of the suggested references.

To the Student

In our experience, work with these cases is best done both individually and in small groups. Individual preparation—reading the case a couple of times, underlining the issues, and developing a basic approach—is recommended before working with a group of classmates, especially as you begin your first cases. After you gain experience, the instructor may have your group read a case and work through it together.

Although you may sometimes struggle as you work through these cases, we encourage you to learn to enjoy the process because it is in this struggle that you will develop and refine personal and professional strength.

Rotella's Guidelines
for Applied Sport Psychology Consultants

The following is a list of core beliefs and values that I have found to be important not only to my personal performance consulting with coaches and athletes, but also to the many consultants I have prepared during the past 20 years.

An effective applied sport psychology consultant
- Is ready to teach when an athlete is ready to learn
- Loves to help athletes go where they couldn't go on their own
- Believes that the magic is inside an athlete and that when the mind is right, an individual's true potential will show in his or her performance
- Realizes that there is no such thing as playing over one's head—moments described in such a way are actually honest looks at one's true potential
- Understands that the mind controls the body
- Realizes that there is very little difference between being "in the zone" and "choking" but that the impact on performance is huge
- Bases his or her teaching on a well-thought-out philosophy
- Realizes that athletes are our customers and that customer service is absolutely essential to letting athletes know that we really care about them
- Values and respects the abilities, needs, and dreams of athletes and coaches as well as the demands placed upon them
- Is an effective communicator
- Loves to listen and understand

Continued

- Loves to teach
- Realizes the importance of mental discipline and taking personal responsibility for one's actions
- Loves to help athletes and coaches seek their fullest potential
- Believes that confidence, concentration, composure, and commitment can be learned and taught because they are simply skills that can be practiced
- Realizes that most of the time people become what they think about themselves
- Realizes that a person's perceptions of him- or herself are more important than the opinions of others
- Realizes that it is possible to have low self-esteem and high self-confidence in a particular sport and that it is also possible to have high self-esteem and low self-confidence
- Understands that sport performance is not all in the head—but that a good bit of it is
- Is never critical of the coach or teammate of an athlete with whom he or she is working
- Strives to teach athletes the advantages of a positive, optimistic attitude over a negative, pessimistic one
- Understands that patience and persistence are usually valued and helpful skills but that it is sometimes best to quit and try a different activity
- Realizes that athletes must learn to do what they love or must learn to love what they do
- Knows that you are either playing to play great and win or playing to be mediocre and not lose
- Teaches that it is impossible to be courageous if at first you aren't afraid
- Knows that athletes must accept that, being human, they will sometimes experience fear and must learn to fight through it and do it anyway
- Realizes that athletes know in their hearts whether they played the way they are capable of playing and that this is ultimately the only measuring stick that really matters

Continued

- Knows the importance of finding out how good you can get and how many of your dreams can come true
- Teaches athletes that competition demands a certain amount of mental toughness and emotional resilience that must be developed
- Knows that there is no one personality common to all great athletes and that all athletes must learn to trust themselves enough to be themselves if they wish to excel (in team sports, this must be done within the restrictions of team membership)
- Realizes that a great sport psychology consultant must never start thinking he or she is smarter than the team's coach
- Never works with an athlete he or she does not believe in or does not think he or she can help
- Knows that a sport psychology consultant must earn credibility from helping athletes and coaches perform at a higher level—an academic degree does not necessarily grant a person credibility in the world of sport
- Knows that it is very difficult to teach others to trust their instincts and have confidence in themselves if the teacher does not trust his or her instincts and believe in him- or herself
- Realizes that long-term success is better than short-term success
- Realizes that process is very important but that most athletes will agree to get into the process because they want winning results
- Knows that it is just as possible to try too hard and care too much as it is to try too little and care too little
- Knows that when you lose in competitive sport, the good news is that tomorrow is a new day that starts all over again at dead even— and that when you win, the bad news is that tomorrow is a new day that starts all over again at dead even
- Knows that athletes either get better, get stuck, or get worse
- Realizes that the better athletes get, the harder it is to get better and the harder it is to maintain a great attitude
- Realizes that anyone can have a great attitude once in a while or some of the time but that it is difficult to have a great attitude all of the time

Continued

- Knows that athletes learn different things about their attitude when facing failure, adversity, and success—but that all are equally valuable experiences
- Knows that athletes must learn the difference between talking about being committed and acting committed on a day-to-day basis
- Knows that you never know when it will all fall in place
- Knows that it is easier to be patient when having fun
- Knows that when competition begins, it is better to be too confident than not be confident enough
- Teaches that when the game is over, it is best to remember that being a great athlete doesn't mean that you are bigger than life, better than life, or more important than life
- Knows that no one does it all alone and urges athletes to remember the importance of friends: Let them help you with your dreams and remember to help them with theirs
- Teaches athletes to be dedicated and to prioritize sport if it is important to them but to not take sport or life too seriously: None of us is going to get out of here alive anyway
- Realizes that sport is a game and that it has to be played
- Knows that it is best to respect the competition but believe in oneself
- Realizes that if there were no competitors, it would be no fun to compete
- Knows that competitors help an athlete get better
- Tries to remember always what he or she is trained to do and to bring in other specialists to do what they are trained to do—it is crucial to see this as a strength rather than a weakness
- Knows that ultimately athletes must take personal responsibility for how they choose to think about and respond to situations in which they find themselves
- Knows that solutions for athletes in team sport situations must be beneficial to both the individual and the team—the athlete has not been forced to play a team sport but has chosen to play on and be part of a team; he or she can always choose to leave the team

Continued

- Knows that commitment on a sustained, day-to-day basis is crucial to turning dreams into reality; those who *only* dream are usually living in a world of fantasy
- Knows that every problem has a solution but that you may have to exert effort and time to find it
- Knows that sometimes an athlete must be given an answer and that other times an athlete should be allowed or guided to figure out his or her own solution
- Knows that sport psychology consultants, as a general rule, should not violate an athlete's confidentiality
- Knows that most coaches honestly care about and are concerned about their athletes
- Knows that team sport athletes must often be helped to enjoy playing roles in a team that are more minor than they would prefer
- Knows that it is crucial to help athletes develop perceptual alternatives for effectively dealing with situations
- Knows that psychology evolved out of philosophy and that therefore it is helpful to teach athletes to have healthy competitive philosophies which will allow them to naturally and effortlessly think better than athletes with unhealthy competitive philosophies. Frequent episodes of jealousy, envy, or anger are signs of a misguided philosophy.
- Knows that participation in competitive athletics should lead to a love of competition, respect and admiration for fellow competitors, and healthy personal development if effective approaches to competition are taught
- Knows that a person has a free will and that therefore every thought is willfully chosen
- Knows that athletes who always claim that they are dedicated, committed, and in possession of a great attitude while complaining about their teammates' attitudes usually *do not* have a great attitude themselves

Case Studies in Sport Psychology

1

ANXIETY AND
AROUSAL

Rotella's Insights
and Observations

Athletes must understand that it is impossible to be courageous if at first you are not afraid. Fear is a natural and healthy human emotion, experienced at times by all competitors. So fear does not separate athletes from one another. Courage, which is the willingness and the ability to feel the fear, face it, and enjoy the challenge of attacking fear and busting through it in important competitions, is what separates champions from others who compete.

A Hole New Ball Game

Cole Kelly

"Oww! You jumped on me!!"

Those were the first words I ever heard out of Donald Anderson's mouth. He bellowed those words at me in 1981 at the YMCA when we were both first graders at different schools. Strange as it seems, that encounter represented the start of a friendship that would grow stronger during the years to come. Donald and I spent countless hours at each other's homes, playing games in the backyard, watching cartoons, and getting into squabbles. Arguments often revolved around who was or was not following the rules of the many games we played. We even had a full-blown fight over whether Babe, my 80-pound black Labrador, could "beat up" Donald's 15-pound poodle.

"Muffin would kill Babe in a fair fight, Ray, and you know it!" Donald screamed, with a tear running down his seven-year-old face.

The basic reality of size and strength obviously did not enter his mind at any time during the argument. I finally relented and said it would be a "tough fight." The routine of arguments and compromises continued throughout our childhood, but the frequency declined as we grew older. Donald's competitive nature, however, never did decline.

Our sport lives also began early and together. Donald's father, Mr. Anderson, was a well-known basketball coach. He persuaded one of the youth team golf coaches to place us on the same golf team when we were 11 years old. Both of our fathers were avid, as well as accomplished, golfers. They agreed we should also play in the summer junior tournaments together if we wanted to go beyond hitting balls and learn to play the game. Mr. Anderson was a confusing man at times, but his intentions were in the right place.

"Ray, this karate class you and Donald are taking is important to y'all's discipline. Once you are done, I could tell you to chop down a tree with your bare hands, and you would do it," Mr. Anderson said one night as he drove us home from class.

3

I never knew whether he meant it as a joke, or if he was serious. I simply smiled and politely agreed, as I still do to many of his comments that I do not fully understand. Mr. Anderson prompted hard work and discipline, and he was never slow to critique our performances while on the practice tee or the golf course.

"You don't chip that ball, you village idiot. Putt it!" That was one of his favorite and most-used sayings then, and one that he still says to me today at times.

As Donald and I settled into our summer, the junior tournaments began. Because my father worked Saturday mornings, Mr. Anderson would take us to the course, and my father would pick us up. Donald was, and still is, a better athlete than me. Unfortunately, Donald's attitude and emphasis on finishing first was a problem even when we first started to play. I remember Donald throwing his golf bag into a stream after losing a play-off for first place.

"Leave them there, Ray! I quit this game. I should have quit after that tee shot on number 5. I just knew I wasn't going to win after that!"

I did not understand what the fuss was all about. After all, Donald had just won a trophy half the size of his driver. It made me smile just thinking about getting a chance to hold the trophy in the car. I didn't say anything, though, and I picked up the bag and carried it in for him. Donald was not reprimanded by tournament officials for his conduct, and he told me it wouldn't happen again. Once in the car, we talked about our rounds. My comments were simple.

"I had fun playing with Scott today. He said his dad was a pro who could probably beat you, Dad. Oh, and could you help me with my putting when we get home? I really need some help," I rattled off to my father.

Donald was still obsessed with the bad drive he had hit off the number 5 tee. "The ball hit the last pinecone on the tree and fell in the water! I was done after that. That ruined my whole round."

My father told Donald not to worry about one shot too much and to try to play each shot one at a time. Unfortunately, this advice went in one ear and out the other.

Before we knew it, we were starting high school. In high school, our social and athletic lives began to blossom. Donald became a very good basketball player, a good golfer, and a complete perfectionist. As teammates on both the football and golf teams, we enjoyed much success. We shared three regional titles and one state championship in football. Donald also became the scoring and inspirational leader on his father's basketball team. As a senior, he led the team in scoring, assists, and, interestingly, technical fouls. He was named MVP for his efforts. As a junior, he helped our golf team win the state championship, an accomplishment that we were expected to repeat the following year. With Donald and me occupying the top two spots on the team, we were considered a lock to repeat. That was not to happen, though, and I will never forget just how we lost both the region and state championships.

In a nutshell, Donald played the worst two rounds of his high school career. It all seemed to start when Donald got upset with the coach when he was asked to play conservatively during the state championship.

"I am going to play great tomorrow, Ray. Can you believe the coach asked me not to take any chances?! I know I played bad at the region tourney, but I'll make something great happen tomorrow. You wait and see."

"The course we're playing tomorrow is pretty tight and can really get you if you hit one off line," I replied. "Why don't we both play to the middle of the greens and just try to make the putts? We do that, and I guarantee you we'll win the team championship."

"No, I am going to charge that course from the start. I'll play well, and you will, too," Donald rebutted.

After making a six on the first hole and a par four on 2, Donald progressively played worse. His only words to me were, "I can't believe I made six on the first hole this morning. You know, if I had holed out with a par, I would have played well. Damn, that six really ruined the rest of my round."

After that tournament, the last high school tourney of our careers, we moved on to graduation and college. I decided on the University of Springfield, where I had a spot on the team, while Donald surprisingly was invited to play on the golf team at the University of Southern Georgia. This was a wonderful, albeit strange, thing that had happened for Donald. Yes, he was a good athlete, but he was never an individual medalist in a major high school or junior tournament. Recruiters consider a golfer's record in these events the most important factor when deciding who they want to sign.

During our first year apart, our friendship surprisingly grew stronger. Each time I returned home, we played golf and hung out together as much as possible. I was happy to hear that college life was going well for him but was dismayed to witness his declining ability and attitude on the golf course. Because of his walk-on status, Donald felt he had to prove he could play to the other players on the team, instead of proving that to himself. As his scores worsened, the head coach began to put more pressure on Donald to improve.

By spring, six months later, Donald's play continued to be mediocre. Donald's coach finally gave him an ultimatum: Complete three rounds of golf with a total score of 235 or lower (a decent score on a tough golf course), or leave the team.

Donald brought his predicament to my attention almost as soon as the coach told him. At first, he did not seem too worried.

"It shouldn't be a problem, Ray. I can play this course that well any day."

I was not as confident. Donald had a history of taking high-pressure situations much too seriously, and these were the most important three rounds of his career. When we saw each other at Easter break, I could see the tension beginning to build in both his words and his golf swing. To make matters worse, Donald's father was going to "help" his son, making the trip back to Georgia to be there for Donald's all-important three rounds.

"You've got to get off to a good start, Son. I don't know what you've been thinking up to this point, but you have to get yourself together," he said abruptly at the driving range one day before Donald's first round.

Donald went out and shot 80 for the first round. The next night he called me to tell me that he had played poorly again and had shot 79. Now he had to shoot a 76 or better, or his college golf career would be over.

"Ray, I don't know how to start this round off. I'm afraid I'll do something wrong on the first couple of holes and blow the rest of my round. And Dad said that if I don't play well I would either have to go to school back home and move in with them or get a job to pay for the apartment at school. Man, I have to do well. What do you think? I need some help, pal, and you're the only one I've got."

"Give Doc, the sport psych guy, a call. A couple of other guys on your team told me he helped them quite a bit. He deals with this kind of thing all the time. I'll bet if anyone can get you ready, he can," I said.

"Sure. I'll try it. I've talked to him casually, and he's a decent guy. Heck, I'll try anything right now. You know how much golf means to me!"

Donald called Doc and arranged to meet the next morning. The two of them sat in the corner of the gym, where Doc asked him how he had decided to call. Donald started telling him about me, and then told the whole story pretty much like I just did. After about seven minutes of straight talk, Donald finished and looked at Doc expecting a miracle.

If you were this sport psychology consultant, what would you do to assist Donald?

Question Guide

1. Describe the characters in this case.
   A. Donald
   B. Ray
   C. Donald's father, Mr. Anderson
   D. Ray's father
   E. Donald's college coach
   F. The sport psychology consultant
2. Describe the main issues in this case.
3. What factors contributed to Donald's poor performance?
4. As a sport psychology consultant, generate some courses of action that might assist Donald.
   A. Training and preparation for the upcoming round of golf
   B. Psychological strategies for dealing with anxiety and heightened arousal
5. How feasible is each course of action?
6. What are the ramifications for Donald of each course of action?
7. As a sport psychology consultant, would you become involved with the relationship between Donald and his father? Why or why not?
8. What would you do to prepare Donald if he has a bad first hole?
9. How would you help Donald deal with the outcome of the third round (success or failure)?

Young Riders

Peter E. De Michele

JEFF PORTER, THE COACH of the U.S. Equestrian Junior National Team, called me from his hotel room in Toronto where his team is about to compete in the Canadian Internationals.

"We're in a tight spot," he began. "We just had a horrible experience at the U.S. Nationals, based on our dismal performances. But that doesn't come as much of a surprise, because the riders are so young and inexperienced."

"What's your experience with them?" I asked.

"I haven't had much time with this team. Just a few weeks ago, Jack Tobbins, the national organizer for the youth riding club, persuaded me to coach them for the U.S. Nationals and the Canadian Internationals. Bill Sanderson, the former coach and legend, retired two years ago. He had a year-round training system in place which produced outstanding riders and was well-known and respected internationally. Since then, some of my teammates from the U.S. National team I was on have chipped in to help coach, at Jack's urging. Don't get me wrong, it's great that they helped out, but there is no regular coach, no training camp, and no consistent preparation. The team is in shambles."

Jeff then focused on how he became their coach.

"No one wanted to take them to the Nationals and Internationals with such inexperience because it is too much of a risk in such a dangerous sport. I've only coached one year at the club level myself. But Jack begged, pleaded, and offered me an enticing sum of money, so I decided to give it a shot. But seeing how we did at Nationals, I'm not sure that was a good decision. I'm not sure I even want to be coaching them," Jeff admitted.

To get a clearer picture of why Jeff is so discouraged, I asked, "What exactly happened at Nationals?"

"All I could think about on our long bus ride to Toronto was how embarrassing our performance in the Nationals was. The first day of competition I walked them through the course three times, explaining every nook and cranny in great detail.

This was their first look at the course, and I talked to them about the terrain, the jumps, the turns, and the way to approach each obstacle. Looking back, I desperately wanted to compensate for their inexperience, so I may have talked too much."

"Maybe," I considered, "but how did they respond?"

"There was a large, noisy crowd gathered waiting for the competition to begin, but my riders looked focused, and seemed to understand what I was saying. That is, except for Elissa, who was looking glassy-eyed at the crowd much of the time. And Jason, the least experienced and least skilled of the bunch, was only interested in the order of the fences. Otherwise, he ignored my coaching. He's been a member of the Junior National Soccer Team and played to much bigger crowds than this. Later, Jason's comment about how small the crowd was for a national event was, 'This is a joke.'"

With time for only a quick breath, Jeff got into what had happened on competition day.

"During warm-up for the U.S. Nationals, Elissa, our oldest and most experienced rider, just lost it. She couldn't remember anything we went over on the course walks. I think she was terrified and frozen at the same time; she looked like she was in a very uncomfortable trance. Six weeks ago, at team trials, she took a bad fall and was hospitalized. Since then she has become the most timid rider on our team.

"Then competition started, and things got worse. Elissa fell off again, just like in trials, and was knocked out for nearly ten minutes. She was inconsolable for hours afterward, and kept talking about how she had let the team down. Two of the other riders forgot the order of the fences and were eliminated for going off the course. Everyone else on the team had one mishap or another, which were major point deductions. Ironically, the only one who rode well was Jason."

"Sounds like a rough time all around," I agreed.

"It was, but I know that Internationals are going to be much more difficult. Since no one on this team has competed internationally, they must not realize how tough international competitions are, 'cause they were excited and making a lot of noise on the bus back to the hotel just now. But I'm afraid for these kids.

"At team trials only eight riders competed for the ten spots. Of the five girls and three boys, Elissa is the only one who is not 16 years old, the minimum allowable age for international competition. She's 18. Two riders just learned how to ride within a year of the trials. They'll all be competing against athletes older than them who have considerably more experience. And experience, more than age, will be a huge factor."

Coach Porter continued to describe how he'd been thinking and feeling two days ago when the bus arrived in Toronto. "As for me, I feel so unsure of how I can help my riders. I just don't know what I could have done differently at the Nationals. Our first night here I didn't sleep. I was so overwhelmed thinking about how unprepared they were. And I kind of know how they feel and what they're up against."

"What do you mean?" I wondered out loud.

"You see, I started out as a timid rider myself. Many times I was hospitalized due to slight miscalculations at high speeds over the large fences in international competitions. But Coach Sanderson helped me gain confidence and strength as a rider through a long process of training and gradually increasing challenges. In Sanderson's system, I started with small challenges like the smaller novice levels close to home. As I progressed, Coach guided me to bigger challenges. Over the course of my ten years, I became a confident and successful rider, and a national champion.

"I was up all night thinking about how these kids just have not had the proper training. That's what scares me. I've told them that the international competition would be much more challenging than the competition in the United States, but I don't think they realize how tough it will be. I don't know, but I think it's just as well they don't know at this point. No sense scaring them now. Right?"

As I kept silent for a moment, instead of responding right away, Jeff took the opportunity to fill me in on what had already happened today.

"So this morning I dragged myself out of bed and gathered the team for their course walk for tomorrow's first day of the Internationals. There were nearly 300 competitors gathered at the enormous first fence. This was the largest number of competitors and the biggest fences the U.S. team had ever seen. The course designer led the athletes through the twisting two-and-a-half mile course, and pointed out the many impressive obstacles. All of the competitors were loud and excited, except our team. We walked along glum and subdued behind the course designer.

"After the official walk, the team, still quiet, got on the bus and we went to late breakfast. They all had glazed expressions while we rode to the restaurant and during the meal. Jason commented to the others about how big the fences were. Nearly everyone looked up and nodded. I didn't say much, but I did my best to be positive and reassuring. That was tough, though, because I definitely have my doubts.

"And when we got back to the hotel, I encouraged them, 'Don't worry, you can do it. We'll walk the course again and I'll show you how to get through it.' They didn't respond, but were silent. Elissa stayed behind and began crying. She said she didn't want to compete."

"I understand the situation you're in," I responded.

"Yeah, well I've been doing all the talking," Jeff replied. "How can you help me with this?"

Question Guide

1. Describe Jeff Porter.
   A. His previous experience as a rider and a coach
   B. His expectations for the team
   C. His current emotional state regarding the team
2. Describe the characters in this case.
   A. Jack Tobbins
   B. Bill Sanderson
   C. Elissa
   D. Jason
   E. Other teammates on the Junior Team
   F. The sport psychology consultant
3. Describe the main issues in this case.
4. What factors contributed to the team's poor performance at the U.S. Nationals?
5. As a sport psychology consultant, generate some courses of action that the coach might elect to follow.
   A. Training and preparation for the Canadian competition
   B. Psychological strategies for dealing with the anxiety of team members
6. How feasible is each course of action?
7. What are the ramifications for the team members and the coach of each course of action?
8. As a sport psychology consultant, would you be more concerned with issues pertaining to the coach or to the athletes?
9. Once this competition is completed, what course of action should Jeff Porter attempt with the team members?
   A. Training and preparation for upcoming competitions
   B. Psychological strategies for dealing with their anxiety

2

INTERPERSONAL
RELATIONS

Rotella's Insights
and Observations

There is little doubt that the ability to get along with others, to support the dreams, feelings, and efforts of others, and to empathize with others are crucial skills in the journey to athletic success. The ability to relate and communicate effectively with teammates, coaches, competitors, support staff, and family and friends is a necessary skill. Some athletes come by it naturally, and others must develop it. If athletes fail to develop skills at relating with others, their athletic development will usually be hindered.

Going the Extra Mile

Fayyadh R. Yusuf

IT WAS THE LAST HALF MILE of the race, and Andrew knew that if he was going to make a move to finish at least second, he'd have to start his kick immediately. As the finish line approached, Andrew managed to break from two other runners and pass the second-place runner in the last ten meters. Excited about his strong finish, Andrew looked for Coach Carter, expecting some expression of congratulations.

As Andrew approached his coach, he sensed that once again his attempts to gain some sort of approval or positive reinforcement had been in vain. Without even looking up or smiling, the coach belittled Andrew's accomplishments and efforts by remarking, "If you started your kick sooner, you would have cut your time."

Andrew was recruited to run track and cross-country at Big University, but the latter was his best sport. Unfortunately, the love and enjoyment Andrew experienced back in high school were not to transfer to his first year of college.

In high school, one of the things that really motivated Andrew to run was his own natural ability. His talents continued to show in the indoor track season and again in the spring outdoor season. Andrew was the star and a favorite of the high schol coach. He had lots of friends for social support, and although running was taken seriously, everyone made sure they also had fun.

It didn't matter whether Andrew was getting ready for a meet or practice, he just looked forward to running. On those rare days when Andrew wasn't motivated to run, he knew that he would at least have the opportunity to be with his teammates. His natural ability, being part of a team, training hard, and having fun were why Andrew loved the sport. With some help from his father, who was also an avid runner, Andrew began attracting attention from a number of colleges.

Over the course of his senior year, Andrew narrowed his list of potential schools down to three. Little College, a Division III school, was always ranked in the top five for cross-country and had the best running program. Midsize University, a Division I-AA school, didn't have a strong running program but offered a better academic environment than Little College. Finally, Big University, a Division I school, offered both solid academics and a running program. Although Big U's cross-country and track teams were not very strong, they did compete in several national events.

Big University sent Coach Ventura to recruit Andrew after he placed in the state finals his junior year. Andrew was really impressed by Ventura's sincerity, not to mention the fact that the coach traveled nearly 12 hours by car just to meet with him. Ventura was a fairly young coach who, as a former collegiate runner, still appeared to be in very good condition. Besides maintaining an athletic appearance, he also came across as very articulate, confident, and down-to-earth. Based on this first impression, Andrew felt like he could trust Ventura as his coach.

Coach Ventura knew that neither of Andrew's parents had gone to college, so he emphasized academics during their meeting. He also assured Andrew that the running program would not consume his collegiate life. Unlike many other sports, runners were allowed some independence in designing their workouts to best suit their schedules.

"Andrew, I think Big U would provide a great environment for both your academic and athletic goals to develop. You'll have your choice of a wide variety of majors. The campus is very attractive, as is the city itself. The community is a tightly knit one, with the university providing many extra opportunities both socially as well as academically. As for athletics, our track-and-field team gets to compete in meets all over the region. You can be exposed to some really great competition without the stress that big-time sports often carry with them. After you visit Big U for yourself, I think you'll agree it is a great place."

Andrew was practically sold on the school. His only reservation was learning that Coach Ventura was taking a job at another school.

"I've decided to leave the university for another job," the coach told him. "Please don't let this fact stop you from wanting to go there. Visit the campus, and then decide what's best for you."

Although disappointed by this news, Andrew still looked forward to going to Big University to compete in a sport he and his father both loved. However, Andrew couldn't help but wonder why a young coach would give up a job and school he appeared to love so much.

After the first few weeks of college, Andrew knew things were going to be different than he had expected—and probably not for the better. He now found himself getting beat by all the other runners every day and even twice a day, and he never felt like a member of the team.

Since there was a small group of freshman who Andrew knew slightly, he always ran with them during their morning and afternoon practices. Although he was glad to have their company while they ran, they didn't get to know each other much, and he also found himself isolated from the older runners. There was very little interaction among teammates, and even his coach was very distant.

Coach Carter had a reputation for not caring about his entire team. Rather, he focused his attentions on those athletes he felt were worthy of his time. At Big U, this meant that the top female runners received the majority of Carter's instruction. Next came the top male runners, followed by "everyone else." Andrew fell into the last of these three categories and consequently had very few interactions with his coach.

At the end of the fall cross-country season, Andrew and Coach Carter had their longest conversation to date. Andrew asked, "Since I did not compete in any races, would it be possible to redshirt this year?" This "extra" season would effectively be an additional semester of college, which Andrew didn't mind so long as, by that time, he had developed into a better runner. Coach Carter agreed with the idea, and the conversation ended almost as quickly as it had begun.

This talk with Coach Carter reminded Andrew of the visit Coach Ventura had made to his house a year earlier. Andrew wished at that moment that Ventura were still around. Ironically, it was about this time that Andrew learned from other teammates that Ventura was forced to resign because he and Coach Carter argued constantly. "They had very different philosophies," said Keith, one of the older runners, "and Carter didn't want to be challenged by one of his assistants." Consequently, new assistant coaches were hired who did no more than act as team managers, catering to Carter's requests.

A few months later, at the end of his first collegiate indoor season, Andrew found himself in a familiar position. He hadn't made a lot of friends on the team, he had only briefly spoken with his coach, and after training all winter, he was not given an opportunity to race and show his coach what he could do.

Now with two weeks off, spring outdoor season practice was about to begin. Andrew would have to go it alone, since his roommate, Jimmy, and another freshman runner, Carl, both quit after the indoor season ended. As Carl explained it, "Coach Carter has taken all the fun out of running and competing. I neither want nor need the stress of dealing with that guy!"

That February, as Andrew prepared for his spring season, he decided that if he couldn't change his coach's attitude, then he'd change his own. Starting the first day of practice, he trained hard and made a concerted effort to get to know his teammates. After opening up to them and earning their trust and respect, Andrew learned that his feelings were not uncommon. As it turned out, many runners were unhappy with Coach Carter, who seemed to take notice only if you did something wrong. Keith once told Andrew, "You could run the best time of your career and Carter wouldn't say a word. Miss one of his stupid practices, though, and he'd nail you as if the whole world were coming to an end."

One year later, Andrew was running in some of the meets. The exposure to competition brought along a lot of ups and downs. One week, Andrew went from a second-place finish to a personal worst in back-to-back meets. Through it all, however, Andrew refused to quit. He stayed motivated and focused on his goal, which was to compete and have fun. In order to prove his commitment to the team and to running, Andrew asked his coach to run him in the Smalltown Relays, an upcoming meet.

When Andrew asked Coach Carter about that race, he was told that there was no more room. Although disappointed, Andrew said, "Okay, but I want to run in any event that does have space." After some discussion, Coach Carter agreed to call Andrew if there was room in any of the events that weekend. Over the course of several days, Andrew never received a call from his coach, and he didn't attend the meet.

The day following the Smalltown Relays, Andrew talked to Gordon, a middle-distance runner who attended the meet. Gordon told Andrew that not only were there other events open, but his specialty, the long-distance race, was open to at least three more runners.

Andrew has now come to you, the sport psychology consultant, with his story. How do you go about advising Andrew?

Question Guide

1. Describe Andrew and what he had hoped to get out of his collegiate career.
2. Describe the other characters' relationships with Andrew.
   A. Coach Ventura
   B. Coach Carter
   C. His teammates
   D. His parents
3. Describe the main issues in this case.
4. Describe Coach Carter's coaching style. How does it affect his athletes' performance?
5. What could Andrew have done differently?
6. As a sport psychology consultant, generate some courses of action that might assist Andrew.
7. How feasible is each course of action?
8. What are the ramifications for Andrew of each course of action?
9. As a sport psychology consultant, would you become involved in the relationship between Andrew and Coach Carter? Why or why not?
10. What types of interpersonal skills and strategies would you suggest to Andrew and/or his coach?

Lanky Lefty

Thomas Johnston

BECKY IS A FIRST-YEAR PLAYER on a nationally ranked women's NCAA Division I tennis team. She is six feet tall with a powerful left-handed serve. Her ground strokes are technically sound, but she makes too many unforced errors. Her volleys are solid, and she moves well for a tall player. As a high school tennis player, Becky always played a great deal in the spring and summer but never practiced in the fall or winter. In addition, she never participated in the junior tennis associations.

In her senior year in high school, Becky won her state high school singles and doubles championships. She was especially dominant in doubles, winning the state finals 6–2, 6–1. It was after these accomplishments that the tennis coach of Major University contacted her about playing collegiate tennis.

Even though Becky was not offered a scholarship, just being recruited by such an outstanding coach and team was very exciting. The summer before school started, she worked very hard on her tennis game. She had never spent much time practicing, but now that she was going to play college tennis, she thought she would devote all her free time to the sport. Each day Becky would get up and run five miles, and then she would do tennis drills for two hours with another local player. After eating lunch, she would go back to the courts and drill again for another two hours. Once a week she would take an hour lesson from the local teaching pro. She looked forward to these lessons because at these times she could focus on the technical aspects of her game. The teaching pro often told Becky that she did not need to worry about her strokes, but Becky felt that if he could make them perfect, she would be unbeatable when she entered school in the fall. She followed this practice routine for the entire summer except for ten days when she went on a family vacation. Missing these ten practice days was upsetting to Becky, but she was still confident that when school started in the fall, she would have no trouble making the starting lineup. Becky knew that no one could have worked as hard on her game as she had.

The fall season was a rude awakening for Becky. Not only did she not make the starting lineup, she did not even make the traveling squad. In addition, she lost every challenge match she played except one. Becky began to feel that maybe she was not such a good tennis player after all. She stopped hanging around with her new college friends because she thought that they would not like her since she was such a "loser."

Compared to the other women on her college tennis team, Becky had very little experience. Most of her teammates had played the junior tennis circuit and had achieved national rankings or, at the very least, sectional rankings. The coach believes Becky is a very talented tennis player, but her lack of experience has held her back. The coach has told her that she is number 9 out of 12 players on the team. As only six players play singles and there are only three doubles teams in a match, Becky is not getting any playing time. She is getting more and more frustrated because the coach tells her she needs more match experience, but she cannot get into the lineup to gain that experience.

When Becky went to talk to the coach about her poor performance, the coach told her that she believed in her ability, but she just needed to keep working hard. The coach also said that when Becky gained match experience she would begin to play much better. She suggested that Becky enter some tournaments on her own in order to gain the needed experience. Playing in tournaments seemed to be a good idea to Becky, but she liked to go home on weekends to visit her family.

Becky decided to work on her game a little harder by devoting all her free time to tennis. Every morning she ran four miles and then jumped rope for 15 minutes before going to classes. In the afternoon she went to tennis practice for at least two hours, after which Becky asked another player to stay after and play for an hour before dinner. If one of the players could not hit, she would ask the coach to feed balls to her. Typically, the coach fed her tennis balls for 45 minutes, and then Becky ran wind sprints on her own for about 20 minutes.

After dinner Becky did her homework for a couple of hours, then she took a study break for an hour and practiced her serve. She believed that if she could make her serve into a "weapon," she would be tough to beat. When she practiced her serve, her goal was to hit 100 serves in one hour. Although she usually felt rushed, she always accomplished her goal. After increasing the amount of hours she spent on the court for six weeks, Becky felt that she was hitting the ball solidly, but she still could not win a challenge match. Although Becky was committed to working hard, she recognized that something was missing from her game.

My role on the team is that of sport psychology consultant and assistant coach. I had been a head coach of a men's tennis team at a small college for five years before moving to Major. I have training in sport psychology through the master's level and have finished my course work at the doctoral level.

One day about three weeks into the spring season, Becky came to me before practice and said, "I need help. I've got no confidence, Coach doesn't believe in me, and I'm not having any fun." We set up a time to talk, and the next day we met in my office. After a couple of minutes of small talk, Becky started talking about her situation. She said, "Coach doesn't believe in me. She says I'm number 9 on the team, but I haven't even played the four players above me in challenge matches. I know that I'm as good as them, and I'm definitely as good as they are in doubles, especially with my lefty serve, my height, and volleys. I know I can help this team.

"Coach said that I would be the first player to play doubles if someone got hurt. But when Lisa got hurt last week, Joan, the number 10 player, took her spot at number 3 doubles. I know that she's a senior and has more experience, but Coach told me I would be the one to play.

"I don't know what to do. It's obvious that she doesn't believe in me. She's caused me to lose all my confidence, and now I just hate going to practice, but I know that I've got to keep practicing to improve. It used to be so much fun. Coach is so unfair. She tells me one thing and then does another. She told me that I'm the most improved player on the team from the fall, but I still don't get a chance. I know I'm a good tennis player, but she just won't play me in a match. What should I do?"

Question Guide

1. Describe the characters in this case.
   A. Becky
   B. Her coach
   C. Her teammates
   D. The sport psychology consultant
2. Describe the main issues in this case.
3. What factors contributed to Becky's poor performance?
4. As a sport psychology consultant, generate some courses of action that might assist Becky.
   A. Training and preparation
   B. Mental training
   C. Interpersonal skills and strategies
5. How feasible is each course of action?
6. What are the ramifications for Becky of each course of action?
7. As a sport psychology consultant, would you become involved in the relationship between Becky and her coach? Why or why not? Is her coach being inconsistent? If so, what could you do about it?
8. What would you do to prepare Becky if she continues to not play up to her expectations?

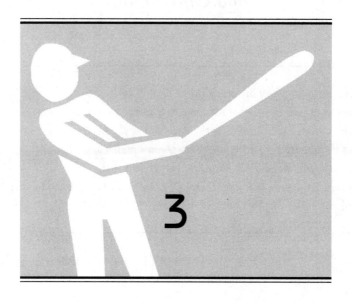

3

TEAM COHESION

Rotella's Insights
and Observations

All athletes who play team sports must always remember that they chose to be a member of the team. Membership was not forced upon them; they agreed to follow the decisions of the head coach as a part of membership. In addition, athletes must realize that their attitudes, efforts, and behaviors toward others either contribute to team cohesion and success or hinder them. This responsibility is taken seriously in championship teams.

Shortchanged at the Track

Peter E. De Michele

State High School had long been a sprinting and field event powerhouse in men's track. For years, they had dominated those events but had been weak in the distances. Last year, Coach Carrie was hired as the cross-country and distance coach, and the team improved under his direction.

Carrie, age 22, had been a state champion miler in high school and had had a decent college career. He earned a position as a teacher right out of college and was beginning his second year of teaching and coaching.

From midway through his first coaching season, Carrie's team looked promising. One runner in particular stood out. Rick was the two-mile state champion in Coach Carrie's first year. His times were not spectacular, but he was nationally ranked and was being pursued by some powerhouse running colleges. Rick was an intense and fiercely dedicated runner. Outside of running, though, he had some trouble. He often slept through classes, which suited his classmates because he was such an arrogant and confrontational individual when he was awake.

Coach Carrie had warned Rick on numerous occasions that his attitude could get him in trouble, but he did not change. Rick was especially fond of taunting the sprinters who were having quite possibly the worst season in the history of the school. There had always been a sort of joking relationship between the sprinters and the distance runners. In previous years, little jabs about how "sprinters are too wimpy to go the distance" and "distance runners are too slow to get out of their own way" were often exchanged, but they were meant in good fun.

Rick, however, took this joking to new obnoxious heights during his senior year. He had become even more arrogant after his championship and often referred to himself as the "sole source" of points for State's anemic team. He was upsetting not only his teammates, but also the head coach.

The head coach, Coach Fielder, had been excellent at the hammer throw in college and had been at State for 15 years. It was under his training that the school had become known as a sprinting and field event powerhouse.

Fielder was frustrated that the team was not coming together the way he wanted. He had some talented individuals, but they were beginners. Many of his best athletes had graduated or were injured. The last thing he needed was taunting from anybody, particularly Rick.

For Fielder, Rick was just another example of the troublemakers on the distance team. Worse yet, it seemed that Coach Carrie condoned this behavior.

Carrie and Fielder had not hit it off when Carrie first arrived, and things had become steadily worse. They had a serious personality conflict, which had facilitated the rift between the sprinters and the distance runners. The two coaches had had a number of heated exchanges on a variety of subjects.

One example of the tension between the two coaches and the athletes occurred the week that Coach Carrie missed practice because of the flu. The head coach took over the practices and told all of the distance runners that they were not to run faster than the slowest runner and that they were not to run more than four miles. They responded by ignoring Fielder's instructions. The runners were disobedient and, consequently, punished each day. These kinds of incidents were part of a history of conflict on the team.

As the sprinting and field events languished, Rick continued to improve and won in distances from the half mile to the two mile. Sometimes he would even run triple events, winning the mile, the half, and anchoring the 4 × 800 for another win. Throughout all of this, Rick continued to torment the sprinters.

Since Rick couldn't seem to leave the sprinters alone and had ignored Coach Carrie's warnings, the head coach created a system of "bear crawls" for punishment. The system was instituted for all troublemakers but was designed with Rick in mind.

This punishment involved waiting for a rainy day. The offender was instructed to crawl on hands and knees for the length of the football field. Up and back counted as one time. Offenders were generally sentenced to five to ten bear crawls for atonement. Fielder kept track of how many each person had earned, and the offenders were called to the field after practice on the first available rainy day.

Every rainy day, one could see men and women, sprinters and distance runners (and always Rick), out on the field, slogging through the muck. Fielder would be there, too, standing in his rain jacket at the side of the field, yelling and blowing a whistle.

Rick had grown tired of the indignity of crawling through the mud and felt he was being unfairly singled out. Coach Carrie had simply rolled his eyes at the idea of bear crawls and told his runners to do them if it would "keep Fielder happy."

After Rick committed one particularly heinous offense (urinating on Fielder's car), the head coach, trying to keep his temper, decided that the bear crawls were not doing the trick. He decided to make Rick run with the sprinters after distance practice.

Rick was incredible. He outran the sprinters across the board. He even showed some talent in the high jump. Rick taunted the sprinters throughout the workouts. He ran to the front and then slowed up so he would be caught. He then sped up and beat them at the end. Rick looked up after these victories and smiled at the head coach.

Fielder was incensed. He could not believe what he was seeing or the way that Rick was acting. Word spread quickly that Rick was destroying the sprinters. The whole distance team was thrilled. They wanted to spend time around the track to see Rick tear up the sprinters, but Carrie managed to keep them away. Instead, the distance runners congratulated Rick in the hallways at school.

Trips to meets soon became segregated. The distance team sat in the back of the bus, and the sprinters and field events athletes remained in the front.

After a while, Rick stopped taunting the sprinters verbally but continued to toy with them during workouts and to look up at Coach Fielder after sprints. This began to bother Fielder so much that he began assigning bear crawls every time Rick looked up at him after winning a sprint. What irritated Fielder even more was that the extra practices with the sprinters seemed to be doing Rick a world of good. His times were dropping steadily in the distance events.

The team was preparing for a large invitational at a major university and was excited to learn that the new athletic director had come up with funds for new uniforms. The uniforms arrived on a Tuesday, and the team tried them on. Unlike the rest of the team, Rick looked upset and was very vocal about not liking the shorts. He said that he wanted to use the ones he had used over the past couple of years. When Carrie asked why, Rick just stammered and said that he thought the new ones chafed too much.

The next day at the practice meet, Rick looked horrible and ran even worse. He was a wreck. After the race he mumbled something about the weather and the shorts bothering him. The head coach smiled and seemed to derive some pleasure from this. Rick asked Coach Carrie if he could please wear his old shorts. Fielder overheard this and said, "You'll wear your uniform like everyone else, or you're off the team."

On the Saturday of the big meet, Rick seemed relaxed and happy. He rode the bus in the back with the rest of the distance runners and was smiling and laughing. They arrived at the meet, and Rick settled in for the long wait for his event. He spent most of his time walking around and stretching. Not only would some of the top talent in the state be in Rick's only event of the day, the two-mile run, but a number of scouts would be watching as well.

Rick began jogging 15 minutes before his event to warm up. He finished his jog and went to the starting line. He took off his sweats, and to everyone's relief, he was wearing the new shorts. As the gun was raised, however, he slid the shorts off and, underneath, were his old shorts.

Rick not only won the race with his best time ever, but he set a school record. He spent a moment talking to a scout and then went to see his family. On the way there, Coach Fielder stopped him and told him it was a great race but that he'd never run for State High School again.

Rick rode home with his parents and stayed away from practice. One week later, he told his best friend on the team, Bobby, to tell Coach Fielder that he would like to come and apologize. Rick walked onto the track before practice with Bobby. Coach Fielder looked up and asked, "What are you doing on my track when I told you that you'd never run here again?"

Rick said, with some difficulty, "Coach, I've come to apologize to you in front of everybody."

Fielder smiled and said, "Well, that's fine. You can if you'd like, but you're never running here again."

Coach Carrie and the entire team looked on in silent disbelief. Rick shook his head and tried to say something, but Fielder raised his hand and said, "It's time for you to leave now."

Rick turned to leave. Bobby, who was the second fastest runner on the distance team, got up and started cursing at the head coach.

"Bobby, you can go, too, if you'd like," said Coach Fielder. Bobby left, and one by one, the rest of the distance team got up and followed Rick and Bobby.

That was the day the coaches invited you to observe practice, but, by ten minutes after four, you and the coaches were the only ones at the track. As he turned and walked toward you, you could already hear what Coach Fielder was going to ask.

Question Guide

1. Describe the characters in this case.
   A. Rick
   B. Coach Carrie
   C. Coach Fielder
   D. Rick's teammates (distance runners, sprinters, field event athletes)
2. Describe the main issues in this case.
3. Describe the coaching styles of Carrie and Fielder. How do their different styles and the strained relationship between them affect the performance and behavior of Rick and his teammates?
4. What could the coaches have done differently?
5. What could Rick have done differently?
6. What effect did Rick's and the coaches' attitudes and behaviors have on team cohesion?
7. As a sport psychology consultant, generate some courses of action that might assist Rick and his teammates.
8. How feasible is each course of action?
9. What are the ramifications for Rick and his teammates of each course of action?
10. As a sport psychology consultant, would you become involved in the relationship between Rick and the two coaches? Why or why not?

Tainted Talent

Terry Marks

"I DON'T KNOW WHAT HAPPENED. I wanted to rip her head off," Tina said excitedly and rather smugly. "It was like all the excuses made for Michelle by her teachers, my parents, other parents, her friends, her coaches, and even by Michelle herself had just run out. I couldn't take it anymore."

Somewhat amused, and comprehending Tina's irritation fully, I inquired, "So, what exactly did you do?"

Tina could hardly wait to give a blow-by-blow account of the confrontation that had occurred at the student-faculty basketball game. I couldn't help letting my mind wander as Tina started from the beginning of her story again. In a strange way, I was proud of Tina, my starting catcher and the captain of the softball team. As I recalled all of Michelle's stunts, her ploys for attention, I was secretly pleased that someone had finally put her in her place. Tina, usually quiet and soft-spoken, was expressing her long-stored frustrations with newfound candor.

"That's when I slammed her up against the wall." Tina went on rapidly, "You know, she'd always pull that rough stuff in practice—the elbows, knees, the push-ing—and then blow up or fake an injury when you started giving it back. I slammed her and said, 'Come on, what are you going to do?'"

By this time, Shalanda and Amy were huddling around Tina, putting in their two cents' worth, high-fiving, exchanging expressions of both approval and dis-belief. They all looked relieved.

Considering my position as assistant coach of the high school softball team, I felt it was my responsibility to act as mediator at this point. I searched for an appropriate response, but my mind was flooded by memories of Michelle's nega-tive behavior. As much as it embarrassed me, I had thought about slamming her myself on occasion.

The first time I saw Michelle's athletic abilities was in a basketball game. Later, I remember thinking, there is a talented athlete wasting a lot of energy glaring at the officials and "mop-balling," which means that she spends a lot of time on the floor and falling down. She just seemed to be very unpleasant around her teammates and her coach.

The second time I saw her was at the elementary school where I teach adapted physical education. She was standing beside her mother's wheelchair, watching her younger brother, Mason, who has Down's syndrome, roll around on the floor in the principal's office. Her father was sitting alone on the couch. What a tough home life I imagined Michelle must have. Strangely enough, though, Michelle's face reflected no hint of distress or hardship on this day. I introduced myself to Michelle's parents as Mason's adaptive physical education teacher. I also mentioned that I would be Michelle's assistant softball coach this coming spring.

Michelle's eyes lit up, obviously pleased. She followed me back to my gym office and was quite talkative, more talkative than I felt comfortable with, having just met her. She confided in me about personal issues that I was not prepared to deal with. Michelle talked openly about herself, her boyfriend, and the softball team and started to put down other team members as if to suggest she was far more talented. I immediately rerouted the conversation in a more positive direction.

"Well, I'm really excited about this spring season. I've heard you gals have a pretty strong tradition in softball," I said.

Thankfully, I was saved by the proverbial bell, and Michelle and I said goodbye as she and I left my office. Two thoughts were immediate as I walked down the hallway. How will I handle this self-absorbed individual in a coaching situation? How will she get along with the other players? At lunchtime, I intended to check with Miss Pratt, the girls' basketball coach, to find out more about her players and who she thought would be on the softball team.

That afternoon, I met Coach Pratt for lunch. She was happy that I had been hired for the softball job, although she expressed her disappointment that I had received the assistant coaching position rather than the head coaching position. That position was filled by a man with no experience with fast-pitch softball, which struck both of us as inappropriate, if not strange.

"I met one of my players this morning," I said.

"Oh yeah? Which one?" Coach Pratt asked.

I paused and zeroed in on her face as I said, "Michelle Stoli."

"What did you think?" Coach Pratt replied with a half smile. She seemed fairly sharp to me, and I'm sure she knew just exactly why we were having this lunch together.

"I really didn't have much to go on. I know Michelle is a pretty good athlete, but something about this morning's meeting just didn't sit right with me." Coach Pratt's expression remained unchanged. I continued, "I was just hoping you could give me a little background on some of my players that you had in basketball."

Coach Pratt went through the list of team members, praising their good attitudes, hard work, and hustling. She even threw out names of parents who were solid supporters of the team. She never mentioned Michelle's name.

I finally cut to the chase. "And how about Michelle?"

All of a sudden, Coach Pratt's face took on a stern and serious look. "I really can't get into it right now. Just be careful. She's got a lot of problems." This was her tactful, professional way of providing a warning without passing any judgment on another person.

I walked back to my gym, dissatisfied with the scant information I had received. Although I anticipated a challenging season, I chose to keep an upbeat outlook. I am an optimist, and I try to reserve judgment until I have all the relevant information in front of me. I was willing to give Michelle the benefit of the doubt.

The first day of practice was in February. It was cold and rainy. Forty-four girls, including Michelle, waited anxiously on the softball field, despite the dreary weather. Tryouts were the normal "weed-and-seed," and I was ready to move forward with the actual season.

During the three weeks prior to our first game, I adjusted to my new position as assistant coach. Mr. Stwodah, the head coach, had not communicated his expectations of me or outlined my responsibilities. Frankly, a lack of organization was apparent, and he possessed neither the skills nor the interest to coach the sport. Despite my opinion of him, though, I never let it affect our professional interaction, and I found my job rewarding because the players were very responsive to me. In particular, Michelle talked to me every day about many different things in her life. She never said she had a big problem or needed an answer, so I mostly listened.

The team started the season impressively, winning the first three games. These early opponents were not all that tough. Many players were not tested under tough situations, and some, including Michelle, played quite mediocre softball. Although we had an athletically gifted team, our softball skills and knowledge of the game would have to improve to beat tougher opponents.

The upcoming week would be a true measure of the team's ability. We had to face three of the top teams in the district. The first game was an away trip to the neighboring county, and the girls seemed very excited. As we boarded the bus, I noticed Michelle was crying. I approached Coach Stwodah and said, "Michelle was crying when she got on the bus. Are you going to talk to her?"

With a sigh and a shrug, Mr. Stwodah replied, "What's new?"

I was incredulous. Apparently, he had no intention of consoling her. I couldn't overlook her distress, knowing that any individual problem could affect the entire team. As I made my way back to Michelle's seat, I was startled to see Michelle no longer crying, but instead laughing loudly and sitting alone in the last seat. I noticed that no one appeared concerned about her outburst. I sat down across from her, guardedly, and said, "I saw you were upset earlier. Is there anything you wanted to talk about?"

Her problem now apparently forgotten, Michelle replied, "It's no big deal. It's a personal problem."

Although I was more than a little perplexed, I respected her privacy and tried to dismiss the incident.

When the bus arrived at the field, there was a definite change in energy among the team. This was a big game. Excitement had turned to anxiety. Their positive, upbeat energy had become nervous energy. Players quickly piled out of the bus, appearing very unfocused. Some were fixing their hair, while others were admiring how their new uniforms fit. A couple of girls were playing with someone's baby brother in the stands. Only three girls were actually stretching and following our usual pregame warm-up.

Eventually, Coach Stwodah commenced the pregame droning that he termed a pep talk. "We're 3–0 in the district. I figure we need to win two of the next three games to give us a good shot at making play-offs." I was astounded. Even the head coach was unfocused. He needed to stress each player's role for today's game. Forget the district standings! Their lack of attention told me that his "pep talk" was ineffective. Over half of the girls never heard a word he said. I understood their inattentiveness since he told them nothing more than to "play together and play hard."

Miraculously, we jumped out to a one-to-nothing lead in the top of the first. In the bottom of the first, Michelle was up to her old tricks. A ball was hit sharply to her backhand side at shortstop. Although she had a great shot at making the play, she missed the ball completely. The left fielder was slow getting to the ball, putting the hitter at second base. Almost at the same instant that the hitter's foot landed on the bag, Michelle hit the ground, grabbing her ankle and screaming. I wondered what happened and asked the player standing beside me in the dugout. Just then, I heard one of the parents behind me comment, "Oh God, there goes Michelle again. She's faking another one."

I looked at Tina, our catcher, who was looking downward and shaking her head. My pitcher was gazing upward, rolling her eyes, while Shalanda and Amy were making eye contact across the outfield.

After it was clear that Michelle was physically fine, the game resumed with her still at shortstop. I was bewildered by what I perceived as everyone's insensitivity to Michelle's discomfort, if not injury. Some minutes later, though, I realized that I was the last to learn that this was just one of Michelle's many ploys to gain attention. We lost the game, but not before Michelle experienced "heat stroke" and verbally berated another player.

My thoughts were jumbled as I drove home that night. How long had Michelle been allowed to get away with this behavior? Why had Coach Stwodah allowed her to remain in the game, considering her unsporting conduct? And how long had these players been subject to her antics? How could this not be affecting the team's performance?

We finished out the season above .500, which put us in the district tournament. Throughout the season, I witnessed many more episodes from Michelle. Realizing that Coach Stwodah had unofficially put me in charge of dealing with her, Michelle soon started seeking out my personal sympathy off the field. There was a fictitious rape resulting in pregnancy and her many lamentations about what others were saying about her behind her back.

At the season's end, I realized that Michelle would be returning as a senior next year. It was a very unsettling feeling. So I just had to call you to explain the situation, and look at what I could have done better last season, as well as what to do next season.

"So, where do we begin?"

Question Guide

1. Describe the characters in this case.
   A. Michelle
   B. Her teammates (Tina, Amy, and Shalanda)
   C. The assistant coach, who narrates the story
   D. Coach Stwodah
   E. Michelle's parents and family
2. Describe the main issues in this case.
3. What factors contribute to Michelle's poor performance on the field and her troubling behavior on and off the field?
4. Describe the different coaching styles of the head coach and assistant coach. How do the two styles affect Michelle's and her teammates' performance and behavior?
5. What could the assistant coach have done differently?
6. As a sport psychology consultant, generate some courses of action that might help the assistant coach in her future dealings with Michelle and the rest of the team.
7. How feasible is each course of action?
8. What are the ramifications for the assistant coach and Michelle of each course of action?
9. Would you become involved in the relationship between Michelle and the head coach, or would you just concentrate on the relationship between Michelle and the assistant coach?
10. How would you build team cohesion?

AGGRESSIVENESS
AND ASSERTIVENESS

Rotella's Insights
and Observations

The healthy display of necessary assertive behaviors is an essential skill in most sports. It is a skill that can be learned and taught. However, it must be taught in a manner that does not lead to unhealthy or hostile aggression in which the aim becomes causing harm to another competitor rather than competing within the rules and striving for victory. Emotions like jealousy, envy, or hate have no place in the development of sport assertiveness.

The Bouncing Ball

Thomas Johnston

CRAIG, A 27-YEAR-OLD tennis coach, is completing his third year as head coach at Major University. Craig played college and professional tennis for two years before an injury halted his career. In each of his three years as coach, Craig believes, the team improved its level of play. In his first year, the team was 13–11 and finished fifth out of nine teams in the conference. Craig was not able to recruit any of his first-year players, because he was hired at the last second when the former coach became ill. In Craig's second year, the team finished with an identical record but moved up to fourth in the conference. The third year of Craig's coaching tenure brought the team its first ever national ranking (16) and a tie for third place in the conference.

Unfortunately, all is not as wonderful as it seems. The best player on the team, the one who the team cannot do without, is Paul, a 20-year-old sophomore. He plays number one singles and doubles for the team. Currently, he is ranked number three in singles and number one in doubles in the country in NCAA Division I. Judging from Paul's junior rankings, this current success has been somewhat unexpected.

Craig recruited Paul during his second year as coach. Paul's father had played tennis for Major University, and this was a big factor in Paul's decision to attend Major. Paul was a highly ranked junior tennis player (85th in the country in the 18-and-under category), and in Craig's judgment he was a great athlete with unlimited potential. Craig's recruiting notes read, "Paul is an explosive and graceful tennis player. He has a powerful serve with tremendous variety. No technical weaknesses are apparent. Paul's ground strokes and volleys are efficient and compact. He can slice and topspin both his forehand and backhand."

Paul has what many would classify as a "tennis body." He is blond, lean, and a little over six feet tall. He is also extremely quick. The rap on Paul, however, is that he is erratic in his play and in his ability to concentrate. This was borne out in his junior record, where he had several wins over players in the top 20 and several losses to players in the 90 to 120 range.

41

Included in the recruiting notes is a comment by one of the players on the team at Major University. He told Craig that "Paul was the kind of player who, if you could hang in there long enough with him, he would eventually fold. The problem is that he is so good that it's hard to hang with him." Although Craig felt that Paul was a calculated risk, he was confident Paul would mature in college and develop into an outstanding tennis player.

During the September of Paul's first year, he and some fellow students became drunk and broke a few dorm windows. Campus police caught them using a long-handled pool skimmer to touch the third-story windows of the women's dorm when they "accidentally" (according to Paul) broke the windows. Paul was brought up in front of the disciplinary committee and was placed on disciplinary probation. He was told that any other problems would result in his being kicked off campus for the remainder of the semester.

The week after Thanksgiving, Paul violated his probation and was forced to find off-campus housing. This time, Paul and the same group of friends found a maintenance vehicle (similar to an electric golf cart) with the keys in it. They were riding it around the streets of the town when they were caught by the local police. Paul and his friends were released to the campus police with a warning. However, Paul was still punished by the disciplinary committee. The terms of his punishment were that he was only allowed to be on campus for classes, to use the library, and to participate in tennis practices and matches. He was strictly forbidden to attend any campus parties or to do anything else on campus. Any violation would result in his expulsion from school.

Paul abided by these restrictions until about halfway through the spring semester. At that point, he was reported to the administration for playing in a pickup football game on campus. Up until then, he had played 12 singles matches and had a record of 9–3. In doubles, he was 10–2, while the team was 8–4 and appeared to be headed for a second-place finish in the conference.

Craig explained Paul's expulsion from school to the team. Although Craig talked to the team about the challenge of playing without Paul, the players blamed their poor showing the rest of the season on Paul. They finished the season 13–11. Craig felt that he should have anticipated Paul's problems and done something to prevent them. He could not help feeling that the team blamed him in some way for Paul's expulsion. Craig also felt a little guilty because his first thought was not for the Paul's welfare, but for the team's win-loss record and how Paul's suspension was going to hurt the team's chances to qualify for nationals.

After Paul's expulsion, Craig started to feel pressure from the administration and from Paul's family. Two days after Paul's semester suspension, Craig received a phone call from Paul's father, Dr. Swanson. He was angry and directed his anger at Craig. He told him, "I trusted you. You knew that Paul might have problems his first year. For God's sake, he's your best player! Why did you let this happen? Couldn't you stop it from happening?"

Craig's first reaction was to get angry with Dr. Swanson, but he held his tongue because the doctor had been very supportive of the team in general. In fact, Dr. Swanson had taken the team to several dinners after matches and had even given the team a ball machine. Although he disagreed with much of what Dr. Swanson was saying, Craig did feel that he could have done something more to help Paul.

The following day, Craig went to his athletic director for advice about Paul and the phone call he had received from Dr. Swanson. The athletic director was sympathetic but offered little concrete advice except to say that the team was probably better off in the long run without the young player. It seemed to Craig that the athletic director was actually happy that Paul was not at Major anymore. This was disturbing to Craig because he felt that the administration should try to help Paul through his difficulties, not be happy to get rid of him.

The next day, Craig decided to have a team meeting to discuss Paul and the rest of the season. During this meeting, many issues were raised, and many opinions were voiced. The senior captain of the team said, "I'm really ticked. We were having the best season we've ever had, and now Paul's blown it for all of us! The season's over!"

Another player, a nonstarter and underclassman, agreed with the captain but said, "Now is the time for us to pull together. Besides, this will just make us better because we'll all have to move up a spot." Most of the players agreed with this sentiment, but Craig could feel their disappointment, and he perceived that they did indeed feel the season was over.

The following year, Paul returned to school. By the end of the season, the team had attained its highest national ranking. Paul avoided trouble with the administration, but he seemed to be acting out more on the tennis court. For example, he would have a quality practice one day, but the next day he would come to practice in a foul mood. By the end of the day, he would have thrown his racket or cursed when his play was not perfect.

This behavioral pattern continued throughout the season and eventually cost Paul the conference singles and doubles titles. During the singles finals, he cursed after double faulting and was given a point penalty. Then, in the second set, he cracked his racket on the ground after missing an easy volley, and the umpire gave him a game penalty. Having already won the first set, Paul was still in control of the match, but it was apparent he was mentally very vulnerable. At the end of the second set, he lost his serve when serving for the match at 6–5. After losing his serve, he hit a ball high into the air, and it ultimately bounced over the fence. The umpire then defaulted Paul from the match because this was his third conduct violation. A very angry Paul stormed away, not even returning for the doubles finals.

Craig calls you, an assistant professor in sport psychology, and asks you what he should do and whether you would be willing to talk to Paul.

Question Guide

1. Describe the characters in this case.
   A. Craig, the head coach
   B. Paul
   C. Paul's teammates
   D. Paul's father, Dr. Swanson
2. Describe the main issues in this case.
3. What factors contributed to Paul's erratic performance and troubling behavior?
4. As a sport psychology consultant, generate some courses of action that might assist Paul.
   A. Training and preparation
   B. Mental training
   C. Training to control aggressive behavior
5. How feasible is each course of action?
6. What are the ramifications for Paul of each course of action?
7. As a sport psychology consultant, would you become involved in the relationship between Paul and his coach? Why or why not?
8. What could the coach have done differently?
9. How would you handle Dr. Swanson if he contacted you to assist his son?
10. How will the rest of the team probably respond if the coach and the sport psychology consultant spend lots of extra time with a player who has let the team down?

The Shy Freshman

Charles Stevens

T HE HORN BLOWS, AND it's tip-off time. The announcer calls out the final starter: "And at forward for Small College, a 5'10" freshman from Tinytown, number 23, Jenn Jordan!" The game is set to begin, and Jenn is jumping center for Small College, a small Division III school that is hosting Crosstown College in women's basketball. Jenn leaps into the air and taps the ball to her point guard, Joan. Joan dribbles the ball down, sets herself, and takes a three-point shot. Jenn is jostled under the boards by Gerry, who is two inches taller and 15 pounds heavier. Jenn backs away, and Gerry pulls down the rebound. Crosstown College pushes the ball up the floor. Jenn sprints back to guard Gerry. When the opposing point guard takes a shot, Jenn makes a weak attempt to box out Gerry, practically handing Gerry the ball and the follow-up bucket.

During the next three trips up and down the floor, Jenn fails to crash the boards and doesn't even attempt to box her player out on defense. Coach Edwards sends in a substitute for Jenn, and as she comes off the floor Coach asks her, "Why aren't you going after the rebound or boxing out?"

Jenn replies weakly, "I don't know. I'm sorry."

Jenn was a quiet standout basketball player at a small high school in Tinytown, located in the South. She was undoubtedly the best player on her team as well as the fastest runner and the best leaper. She led her team in scoring with 18 points per game and was second in rebounding with seven rebounds per game. According to Jenn's high school coach, Coach Smith, Jenn did not have to "muscle" anyone because she could outrun or outjump everyone. He said she loved to play basketball, but she was just shy and sometimes reserved among her peers and coaches.

Throughout her senior year, Jenn was recruited by many Division III schools, some Division II schools, and two small Division I schools. However, Jenn wanted to go to a school that was relatively small and close to home. According to Jenn, that would fit her personality. She had received a lot of attention from many coaches, but she had enjoyed talking with Coach Edwards the most and really liked the personal atmosphere she felt when she visited the campus.

While Coach Edwards was recruiting her, Jenn rarely had much to say. Coach Edwards talked extensively to her about Small College and tried to prompt questions, but Jenn always said, "I don't think I have any questions." After a few more similar conversations with Jenn, Coach Edwards began to wonder about her decision-making ability and her mental toughness. He also wondered if she would fit in with the team and if this would be the correct school for her. Nonetheless, Coach Edwards was pleased when Jenn decided on Small College.

When she arrived at the college, Jenn was well disciplined as a result of the conditioning program she had begun over the summer. As team conditioning began, Jenn worked hard and displayed her athletic abilities by regularly coming in first in sprints and distance runs. Jenn was still shy and reserved, even after four weeks. Coach Edwards noticed it wasn't until preseason practice began that Jenn finally started to mingle more with her teammates. He attributed Jenn's shyness to being a freshman who was learning to find her place.

During the course of the preseason, Coach Edwards had three conferences with Jenn, as he did with everyone on the team, about her goals and hopes for the upcoming season. Each conference was a progressive talk about expectations and how each player was doing thus far. During the conferences with Jenn, Coach Edwards usually got the same responses to his questions, "I just hope I play some, and I really don't know what else to expect. I'd like for us to win, and I'd like for everyone to do well." Coach Edwards was pleased with her concern for the team, but he wondered why she didn't seem very enthusiastic about getting playing time for herself.

As practices got under way, Coach Edwards and Assistant Coach Barry, a female assistant, were impressed with Jenn's ability to work well on her own and with the skill she displayed during individual drills. However, when the team scrimmaged, Jenn didn't seem very assertive. She didn't attempt to make contact to box out her opposing player on defense. When she was playing offense on the inside, she didn't try very hard to get position. The defender would bump her and get the position without much resistance from Jenn. In loose-ball situations, Jenn would watch rather than go after the ball. When she had an opportunity that involved physical contact, she would hold back or retreat.

This lack of effort and assertiveness got Coach Edwards pretty ticked. During one practice in particular, Coach yelled at Jenn, "Jenn, you can give a better effort than that! You've got to give me 100 percent in practice!"

Jenn shot back, "Yes, sir!"

For the next five minutes, Jenn outhustled everyone for rebounds and loose balls; however, she was still not banging the boards as Coach Edwards expected.

After the scrimmage, Coach Edwards told Coach Barry to go to the other end to work on rebounding with Jenn and the two other post players, Tonya, a junior, and Bette, a freshman. The drill was set up so that all three were to go for the rebound at the same time. In this drill, players need to use their bodies to get in good position to get the ball. Jenn got four rebounds out of the 25 shots taken by Coach Barry. Most of those rebounds, though, came right to her without her needing to get in position.

Tonya won the drill, so Jenn and Bette had to run wind sprints. After the sprints were completed, Coach Barry asked Jenn, "Why didn't you get in there and fight for those rebounds? If you would get in there, work for the position, and use your leaping ability, you'd get a lot of rebounds."

Jenn mumbled, "I don't know. I guess I don't want to get hurt."

The coaches talked about what Jenn had said. Coach Edwards said, "I'll talk to her about it and see what she says."

After practice, Coach Edwards asked Jenn, "Why are you afraid you'll get hurt boxing out for rebounds?"

Jenn hesitated, "I don't know. I guess it's because of all the contact."

Coach Edwards responded, "Well, to box out and rebound effectively, you've got to make contact. We'll keep working on rebounding so you can get used to making contact, all right?"

Jenn said, "Okay."

As Jenn left practice, Coach Edwards noticed she continued to be shy around her teammates. Just then, Katie and Val, the two senior captains, came out of the locker room. Coach Edwards asked them, "How is Jenn around other students on campus? Does she have any friends?"

They didn't know about any of her friends or if she had any, but they did tell him that she didn't mingle much with other students. This concerned Coach Edwards just as it had when he first recruited Jenn.

As Coach Edwards was leaving the gym, he bumped into Dr. Hags, one of Jenn's professors. Coach said, "Hey, Dr. Hags, I've got a question for you. I see that Jenn is doing well in your class, but does she participate much?"

"Yes, she is doing well, but she never speaks up in class," answered Dr. Hags. "In fact, her adviser, Ms. Davis, told me that Jenn hardly participates in any of her classes but that she is doing the work. I wish she would speak up more. I think she would do even better."

Coach Edwards turned around to go back inside the gym just as Danielle, Jenn's roommate, was coming out. He asked her, "Hey, Danielle, is everything all right with Jenn?"

Danielle replied, "I don't think so, Coach. Something must be up with her because she isn't eating like she normally does."

Coach Edwards asked, "What do you mean?"

She explained, "Well, today she didn't eat breakfast or lunch. She just got something to drink. For dinner, she only ate two pieces of toast."

"Is there something going on at home?" wondered Coach.

"I don't think so," said Danielle. "It might be some sort of image thing. She seems to spend a lot of time looking at herself in the mirror and complaining about being too muscular."

After his conversation with Danielle, Coach Edwards caught up to Coach Barry in the gym and told her what Dr. Hags and Danielle had said. They both wondered if there was something going on in Jenn's life or if, in fact, it was an "image thing" that was causing her lack of assertiveness. They agreed that Jenn possessed the ability to be an outstanding player at this level, and they could see why she had been so heavily recruited. However, they also agreed that Jenn lacked the desire, assertiveness, and "drive" to be that outstanding player.

The coaches went back to the office, where Coach Edwards calls you, a sport psychology consultant whom he met at a recent coaches' conference. He explains the situation with Jenn and asks, "What would you recommend?"

Question Guide

1. Describe the characters in this case.
   A. Jenn
   B. Coach Edwards
   C. Coach Barry
   D. Jenn's teammates
   E. Jenn's roommate, Danielle
   F. Dr. Hags
2. Describe the main issues in this case.
3. What factors contributed to Jenn's nonassertive play in basketball?
4. As a sport psychology consultant, generate some courses of action that might assist Jenn.
   A. Training and preparation
   B. Mental training
   C. Training to become more assertive
5. How feasible is each course of action?
6. What are the ramifications for Jenn of each course of action?
7. As a sport psychology consultant, would you become involved in the relationship between Jenn and her coaches? Why or why not?
8. What could the coaches have done differently?
9. Might Jenn have a more serious problem than a lack of assertiveness?

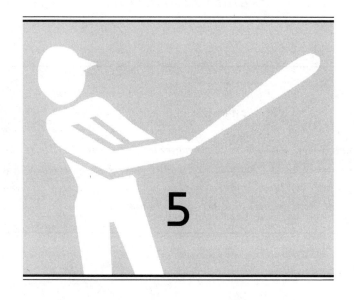

CONFIDENCE

Rotella's Insights
and Observations

Many athletes ask which comes first, the chicken or the egg—confidence or success? The answer is confidence. If you had to win before you believed you could win, no one would ever win for the first time at any level. Confidence comes naturally to some athletes. Those who do not come by it naturally or readily must work on developing it through mental training. Confidence is perhaps the most essential of all the skills needed to become a champion.

The Big Break

John F. Eliot

 ART JOGGED OFF THE FIELD from his position in center only to greet the furrowed brow of his coach. He heard a glove slam into the dugout wall, and the pitcher slumped past him with his head hung. Art looked around at his teammates. Anxious beads of sweat rolled down their dirt-streaked faces. One of the younger players began to unlace his spikes. Art stole a quick glance at the scoreboard. His team was down by two runs in the bottom of the last inning of the Maine state high school baseball championship. For the seniors, this was their last and only chance at a championship jacket.

The air was heavy with tension, yet Art was anything but nervous. The 6'2" junior held all the state hitting records—every single one in the book. Even though it seemed like his team had given up, Art was the picture of confidence. The corner of his mouth cracked into a smirk, showing everyone just how confident he was and how much he was loving this moment.

"Hey, fellas. We're in the *state finals*. You gotta love it. I mean, look at all those fans out there holding up banners for us and screaming their heads off. We're gonna win this thing, and all those great-looking girls are going to go crazy. I love it!!!"

A brief silence was followed by the nodding of heads. First Derek, then Jamie, then Pogs seemed to become infected by Art's attitude and enthusiasm. The players were at the top of their order, and Art was due up third. A lead-off single by Stein followed by a walk to Mike put two guys on for Art.

As Art strode to the batter's box, adjusted his helmet, and gripped his Easton Black Magic, the crowd rose to its feet. All eyes were on him. Art looked around and swallowed the excitement. Taking a deep breath, he tasted the dusty air. One practice swing, then two, and Art dug into the batter's box.

"Come on Artie, we need this one, babe," he heard his coach say. "And, when you get me a dinger . . . I'll make you captain."

Artie's smile widened. He loved all the trust his coach had in him. He stepped out, looked back, and winked in complete confidence. Then he looked into the stands to see his dad beaming from ear to ear. He caught sight of a group of girls in the outfield bleachers holding up a sign that read, "HIT IT HERE FOR A KISS, ARTIE." Practically chuckling out loud, Art thought to himself how wonderful it was to see and hear his name all over the place. He turned his gaze to the frightened pitcher and again grinned a full-of-himself grin. It took only one pitch to decide the game. A fastball right down the pipe and crack, it sailed deep over the center fielder's head.

That night, Art's hometown celebrated—all 500 residents. Everybody he knew, and even people he didn't know, came up to him and marveled how he'd won the championship for them. They gave him presents and hugs, kisses, and congratulations. As his coach promised, Art was named next year's captain. The celebration seemed to last forever. Art felt on top of the world.

The following year passed with a similar flare. Art's skills brought another state championship, a beautiful girlfriend, and an offer to attend the University of Texas to play baseball on a full scholarship. Life, it seemed, couldn't be better.

When Artie got to college, baseball was already under way. The team had practiced for two weeks before the freshmen recruits arrived. Art was extremely excited. He was handed a uniform, a bag full of practice gear, and his new cap. He was told to be on the field by one o'clock.

"Wow," he thought, "this is the big time. These guys are serious."

He went into the locker room to change. There, 25 other guys were busy getting ready, some joking, some stretching, a couple of guys wrestling. Art wasn't sure he'd ever seen guys quite this big.

Throughout the first practice, Art was shuffled through one drill after another. He felt quite lost, and the head coach, a tall, fit-looking man with a squared-off jaw and a cap always tipped down over his forehead, never said a word to him. In fact, Coach Bull Flipman rarely spoke to anyone but the seniors. Art quickly discovered that Coach Flipman's practices were just like his personality—cold, hard, and unrelenting. Nobody stopped to chitchat; nobody was ever idle.

Over the next few weeks, practices continued in the same military fashion. Art found himself making some errors, and he struggled to keep his hitting sharp. As much as he tried to focus on his skills, he couldn't help but wonder why the team was so impersonal. Getting to know the team veterans, who seemed to enjoy wind sprints much more than they enjoyed joking around in the clubhouse, was a slow process. What wasn't slow was Art's discovery that the player ahead of him in each practice drill was the team's prized center fielder.

As the fall season unfolded, Art found himself sitting on the bench a great deal. In fact, despite all his hard work in practice, he had not yet seen any game time. Texas rolled over its opponents, defeating them by large margins, and still Art did not play. Each game, he watched the sophomore outfielder play with more and more awe. Bobby Bean was very good, very quick, and he never seemed to miss at the plate. During batting practice, Bobby launched pitch after pitch into the left-field bleachers. On the rare occasions that freshmen also got to take some batting practice, Art had difficulty concentrating. He swung through most of the pitches and hit weak grounders with the rest. He couldn't help being distracted by mental images of Bobby's hits caroming off the aluminum seats in the stands.

Quite often Art found himself thinking, "I wonder why the coaches brought me here to play with all these pro-prospects around?"

At night, Art frequently fell asleep thinking about all the great plays he'd seen the older guys make. He envisioned Bobby diving full speed across the turf and miraculously stabbing the ball out of the air. He heard the crowd roar, and his heart sank heavily in his chest. Art missed having somebody cheer for him. He felt very discouraged and very homesick.

The fall season came to a close. Art's stat sheet was clean. No hits, no walks, no at bats. His grades did not turn out too well either. Frustrated, Art returned home for the holiday break. His girlfriend decided to date somebody else. His old high school coach was busy and didn't have time to spend with him. He tried to get some workouts in, but he ended up only going through the motions. Home just wasn't the same as it used to be; his life just wasn't the same anymore.

In January, Art flew back to Texas, and shortly thereafter, spring training began. Once again, Art faced long, dry practices. With an important season coming up and talk of the College World Series floating around campus, baseball became anything but fun. As in the fall, Art found himself working extremely hard in practices with no attention whatsoever from Coach Flipman. When the games began, Art again sat on the bench and watched his new idol, Bobby Bean, tear up the league.

At one point, Bobby was awarded Division I Player of the Week, and during the college reception, Art heard Bobby joking to a girlfriend, "It's so easy to get awards like this when you're born with so much talent!"

As the season passed, Art tried harder and harder to improve his skills, but after each game in which he did not play, he would slowly walk back to his dorm with his head down, thinking, "If only I were still as good as I was in high school."

Back at his dorm, he would be greeted by his roommate and stories of how his roommate had won this soccer game or that one, and how his roommate was going to get to travel here or there. His roommate was an All-American soccer player who had helped turn the failing Texas program around. He was also a very charming blond fellow adored by many of the young college women.

"It's just not fair," thought Art. "He's a freshman too, but *he* gets to star in all kinds of soccer games, and the girls love him because he plays. Why am I so horrible? A darn Gatorade cooler does more on the bench than I do!"

For weeks, Art debated quitting the baseball team. He was tormented over the decision. Although he told himself many times that he would finally give it up and just quit, Art desperately wanted one chance, just one chance to prove himself. With two weeks remaining in the season and Texas in contention for a trip to the College World Series, Art got that chance.

The day began just like any other game day. Art quietly made his way to the clubhouse, changed without a word, and headed for his well-worn spot on the bench. Texas was playing Arizona State. Going into the bottom of the ninth inning, it was a tied ball game. The first eight innings were a roller coaster of excitement, with the lead changing four times. The spectators were on the edge of their seats. Bobby was due up. He grabbed his stick and started to head for the plate. As had become custom, Bobby patted Coach Flipman on the butt and tipped his cap to the fans. As usual, Art watched intently, and in awe.

Bobby's spikes clicked on the cement dugout steps, and Art watched as everything turned to slow motion. Bobby's toe twisted off the top step, his foot turning inward. Trying to maintain balance, he shifted his body but came slamming down with all his weight over the twisted ankle. Time snapped back to regular speed, and Art saw Bobby's face cringe with anguish.

"Ahhhhhhh, my ankle," Bobby cried out.

The dugout became a flurry of chaos, no one too sure of what had just happened. Art watched as teammates swarmed around the injured player. Confusion reigned for a few minutes before the trainer announced that Bobby would have to be taken to the hospital. He had broken his ankle.

Coach Flipman, with a rather panicked look, turned to his assistant and shouted, "Marty, do we have anyone who hasn't gone in yet?"

Marty replied, "Just Art, Bull."

His mind still clouded by what had just transpired, Coach Flipman fumbled for some words and spit out, "Well, ah, get him a bat then. . . . And, ah, tell him to hit the ball, or somethin'."

Art's big chance had arrived. Not surprisingly, he was startled as a bat was shoved into his hands. He stepped out of the dugout into a packed stadium and approached the plate in a daze. Thousands of thoughts raced through his head.

"What do I do in this situation? I've never hit college pitching. I've never even been in a college game."

As Art stepped into the box, he tried to focus on the pitcher, but his thoughts wandered. "Can I touch this pitching? . . . Oh boy . . . I don't want to strike out in front of all these people. . . . What if I blow this chance in front of the coach? . . . Oh boy . . . oh boy."

The pitcher delivered a pair of 96-mph fastballs right past Art. "Strike one, strike two." More thoughts rushed through his head. "Uh no, I'm in the hole 0 and 2. He may throw anything on this next pitch."

The pitcher came to a set, the crowd silenced, a bead of sweat dripped off Art's nose. Art fidgeted with his grip. A hard slider came hurling in, and Art tried to swing, but as the ball spun away from him, he only struck air. "Strike three!"

The game screeched to a halt. Artie dropped his head and began the long trek back to the dugout amid shouts from the badgering fans. "You stink!" "Way to help the team!" "Where did you learn to hit?" "Go back to high school!"

His teammates did not say much. Most were just packing their gear. The coaches headed for the clubhouse without a word. Art packed his own gear, did not bother to shower or change, and left the stadium.

Later that afternoon, Art comes into your office with a bunch of concerns: Why did that happen? What would everyone say? What would happen tomorrow at practice? What if they expected him to replace Bobby in the next game? How would he explain this to his roommate? To his friends? To his dad? What would he do? Would he ever be able to regain the self-confidence he once had in high school? And as he looks up at you from his slumped position in the chair, he is clearly hurting. As the sport psychology consultant, what would you say to Art?

Question Guide

1. Describe the characters in this case.
   A. Art
   B. His high school teammates
   C. His high school coach
   D. Coach Bull Flipman
   E. Bobby Bean and Art's college teammates
   F. Art's college roommate
2. Describe the main issues in this case.
3. What factors contributed to Art's poor performance in baseball?
4. As a sport psychology consultant, generate some possible courses of action that might assist Art.
   A. Training and preparation
   B. Mental training (concentration and self-confidence)
5. How feasible is each course of action?
6. What are the ramifications for Art of each course of action?
7. As a sport psychology consultant, would you become involved in the relationship between Art and his coach? Why or why not?
8. What could the coaches have done differently?
9. What could Art have done differently?
10. How would you help Art prepare for the rest of the season (successes and failures)?

The Messenger

David Belkin

 LAMAR CAME INTO MY OFFICE yesterday. It seemed like he wanted to talk. I've been the assistant coach at NPU for six years, and Lamar has been on the team for the past two. He sat down and started to talk seriously a couple of times, which for Lamar is a switch, but then he stopped himself. He never really got around to saying much of anything. I was just as glad; I don't know what I would have said to him anyway. I know he'll come back. That's why I called you; I just don't know what to tell him.

I'd better back up. Lamar is the kid who got in the car crash after our basketball season ended. He was a sophomore this year, and he had really started to shine. He started the season as the ninth or tenth man, and by the time the NIT rolled around, he was first off the bench. He was getting about 20 to 25 minutes per game at two guard and small forward and was averaging a little over ten points per game. He was definitely starting to feel good about himself on the court again.

His freshman year was tough for him; he didn't realize how good the other players were and didn't get much playing time. You could tell that he was pretty depressed, but he put on a good show for everyone. That's why it was so nice to see him feeling good again. Toward the end of the season, Lamar came into my office every couple of days just to brag about himself. He would actually bring in the newspaper and read the headlines: "Lamar Washington had another stellar defensive performance, holding their big scorer to 3 for 10 shooting" or "Lamar Washington hit the crucial basket when it seemed that things were starting to go downhill." Sometimes the smile on his face was so wide that he could barely read. I really enjoyed it when he came in; we had a lot of good laughs together. After he hit that last-second shot to win the Pitt game, he was almost unbearable; he began cutting out article after article and putting them on the walls of my office. He even started talking about the NBA again, just like when he came here as a freshman, and he might have even started to believe it.

It was quite an adjustment for Lamar to come straight out of Bed-Stuy, the worst part of Brooklyn, to this rural, ultra-white atmosphere. This area is 98 percent white and very racist. Neither his high school coach, who never had a player play in college, nor his mother, who worked all the time, gave Lamar much help thinking through his college choice. And he had no other close family or friends to give him advice or support.

I guess he came to me for all the positives because Coach Waters, the head coach, is not a very reinforcing guy and not a real easy person to talk to. All of the black kids, especially the ones from poor, urban neighborhoods, tend to have a hard time with him. He's old and stodgy and really set in his ways. He doesn't let them express themselves on or off the court, and he rarely shows affection for them. The only time he gets emotional is when he's angry. Kids like Lamar have had a really tough time relating to him.

Lamar wasn't a bad kid, despite all the things he might have gotten into in Brooklyn. He wasn't a great student, but he got by. I think it was because he was so likeable. He used to tell me stories about how he could convince his teachers not to fail him just by making them laugh. I think that's how he avoided most of the gang stuff and the drugs, too. He's a loose, carefree kind of person, which really doesn't sit well with Coach Waters. Even when Lamar worked hard in practice, he was still cracking jokes or smiling. Coach Waters doesn't seem to like that much.

Lamar was on a natural high at the end of the season; everything seemed to be looking up. Even his mom got a raise. That's why it was so sad when he got hurt. Lamar and a football player were driving and went off the road, flipped over a couple of times, and went into a ditch. Medical experts on the scene weren't sure if he was even going to make it. I went to the hospital that night, and he didn't seem to be too badly hurt. He wasn't too shaken up, just somber. I kept expecting him to crack a joke, tell me that his crash should be on ESPN, but he didn't. I had never seen him like that before. In a very serious manner he kept talking about how messed up his leg was.

I went back the next morning, and his mom was there. She was concerned but didn't seem very attuned to what he must be thinking. And Lamar was cracking jokes again more than ever. I think he wanted her not to worry, but it was pretty easy to see through him. The doctors said that he had a degenerative hip problem, similar to Bo Jackson's condition. They didn't think he would need a replacement, but they told him that he would probably never be able to play ball again on a competitive level. He wasn't really upset when they told him; I think he just didn't believe them. The thought was probably inconceivable.

He started rehab a couple of weeks later, telling anybody who would listen that he was going to be back on the court. For the first couple of weeks, people would ask him how he was doing and how rehab was coming, but then they stopped. When Lamar told me about that, he said that people were forgetting about him. I think that really bothered him.

It's been about five months, and Lamar is still doing rehab. I'm not sure how hard he's working, but he seems to be making some progress. I saw him playing around on the court yesterday. He's nowhere near what he used to be; you can see him drag his leg every time he tries to pivot or slide, and his quickness is all but gone. I don't know how much better he can get, but the coach has already told him that he "doesn't have a shot in the world" of making the team again. It's been getting tougher for him as the season approaches; all his friends on the team are out playing ball, and he spends most of his time wishing he could be out there playing at their level. I'm sure he misses the individual glory, but I think that he also really misses just being a part of the team. He maintains that one day he'll be back, but I don't know how realistic that is. He gave up on the NBA but hasn't given up on playing with the team again.

Lamar keeps saying, "If Bo can do it, so can I." The only problem is that even though his injury was worse, Bo didn't play basketball. I don't know what to tell him. I don't think that Coach's comment made much difference to him; he told me that Coach Waters never believed in him anyway. If I told him that he was being unrealistic, I think it might mean more, but I wouldn't want to take away his dream. Then again, if it's not attainable, am I just prolonging the agony by not telling him? Maybe I should talk to his doctors.

I called because I wanted you to help me figure out what to say the next time Lamar comes into the office. As a sport psychology consultant, what would you say to Lamar to help him?

Question Guide

1. Describe the characters in this case.
   A. Lamar
   - His personality
   - What he is going through
   - His relationship with the assistant coach (the narrator)

   B. His college teammates
   C. The assistant coach
   D. Coach Waters
   E. Lamar's mom
2. Describe the main issues in this case.
3. As a sport psychology consultant, generate some courses of action that might assist Lamar.
   A. Help him get a grip on reality
   B. Mental training (confidence)
4. How feasible is each course of action?
5. What are the ramifications for Lamar of each course of action?
6. As a sport psychology consultant, would you become involved in the relationship between Lamar and the assistant coach? Why or why not?
7. What can the coaches do?
8. What could Lamar do differently?
9. How would you help Lamar prepare for the rest of his life with or without basketball?

6

EXPECTATIONS
OF OTHERS

Rotella's Insights
and Observations

It is burden enough to live up to one's own expectations without trying to live up to the expectations of others. But other people's judging an athlete's performance and comparing it to their expectations goes with the territory in sport and therefore must be willingly accepted. Athletes who think it is a tremendous burden to be labeled as having great talent and to have great things expected of them should take time to consider the opposite scenario. It would be far worse to have others think an athlete had so little talent that they expected little, and the chance to compete was never given. This perspective is very helpful to learning to appreciate and enjoy one's talent.

The Weight of the World

Jana L. Maas

 Sᴀᴍᴍʏ ᴡᴀꜱ ʜᴏᴍᴇ ᴏɴ ꜱᴜᴍᴍᴇʀ break from college when her
former high school basketball coach called to see if she wanted
to play some basketball with his current team. "Sure, Coach,"
she said. She would never pass up a chance to play basketball.
Sammy had always liked Coach Williams, and she couldn't wait to go play.
Sammy immediately went to her closet and pulled out her beat-up old white
sneakers and fished around for an extra pair of socks.

Coach Williams was a nice guy. Teaching kids to play basketball was what
brought him the most joy. He knew the game of basketball, but he never seemed
to have control over his team. His practices were run by the team instead of him.
The girls would tell him how long they wanted a drill to last. When they were
tired and wanted to stop, they would tell him they had had enough. Maybe he
was too concerned with having all his players like him.

Upon arriving at the gym, Sammy saw at least seven people she had never seen
before. But Coach Williams's 5'3" frame and perpetual smile looked the same
as always. Twelve years of coaching had taken their toll on his now balding and
gray hair. For Sammy, it was a great treat to see her old coach again; it had been
about a year since she had last seen him.

Upon spotting Sammy, Coach Williams jogged over to her. As they talked,
he began giving Sammy brief résumés on the girls, especially a 6' blond girl
named Katherine. She had been a varsity starter since the middle of her freshman year and was supposed to be outstanding. Sammy only knew Katherine by
a paragraph in the papers. "Well, Coach, I came to play some ball. Let's get
going," Sammy said with a smile and a laugh.

It was decided that Sammy would guard Katherine. As they began playing,
Sammy was struck by Katherine's strength. She was tall, but her arms lacked
muscle definition, so she didn't look that strong. "Gosh, she's pushing me all
over the place," Sammy thought as they scrimmaged. "She's taking up a lot of
space and wants the ball, and she's killing me on the boards."

It was a hard-fought battle that evening between Katherine and Sammy. It quickly became evident to Sammy that Katherine was naturally a very talented player but had plenty of room for improving her fundamentals. "She's tough, but she has to know what to do with the ball after they feed it in to her," Sammy concluded to herself. A post person shouldn't let the ball get swatted away by a little guard.

After they finished playing, Sammy approached Katherine to see if she would be interested in learning some advanced post player moves. With a smile, Katherine quietly answered, "Sure."

On only the first day of seeing Katherine play, Sammy felt she was a dream player. Katherine seemed to be willing to try anything to improve her game, and she was very intense about her basketball. "Unfortunately, I won't be able to help her any more this summer," Sammy thought, disappointed. "They have their summer league games, and I work when they practice. At any rate, Katherine's going to have a great year."

A year passed, and Sammy was home for six months because she had taken a semester off between college and graduate school. She decided to get in touch with Coach Williams to see if she could help coach the team. He said he would love it, and Sammy could start as a volunteer assistant coach when the season began in November.

As November and the first practice were approaching, Sammy began questioning her decision to assist Coach Williams. "What if the players don't like me, or I have no idea how to coach?" she thought. "I'll give myself a couple days, and things will be great; they always are. I'll just be glad to get the first couple of practices out of the way. At least I met some of the kids in the summer. Oh heck, Sammy, you're going to have a great time. Quit worrying about it!"

A few days passed, and Sammy *was* having a great time. The greatest part of being the volunteer assistant coach was that she got to work with the varsity team and got opportunities to play on occasion. Working with Katherine a lot the past couple of months gave Sammy the opportunity to get to know her better, as a person and as a player.

As great as all of this was, Sammy sometimes found it difficult to separate her roles as coach and friend. Sammy had to catch herself a few times from being too much of a friend to Katherine in practice. A couple of times they started joking around while Coach Williams was trying to explain plays to the team.

One day before practice, Katherine told Sammy, "It sure is nice to have someone around who understands me." Sammy appreciated the compliment and believed that Katherine was serious about her game, too.

The first couple months of the season passed. League games proved beneficial for the team, and for Katherine in particular. She was averaging 19 points and seven rebounds per game. The team had lost only one game when the new year rolled around. Just then, as the old year exited, something peculiar happened. Katherine's attitude changed drastically. She seemed distraught and tired, and she was not playing up to her abilities. It was as if her intensity were on vacation and she was just going through the motions.

One January evening stood out in particular. The snowflakes were coming down like maple leaves—real basketball weather for the North. It was the kind of night most people would want to stay inside. Fans in Lakeland, however, took their basketball very seriously. It wasn't uncommon to see snowplows on the roads on the way to the game. The blizzard made the trip to the gym difficult, but die-hard fans would brave anything to get there.

Late in the game, Sammy glanced over at Katherine on the bench. Katherine was on the verge of tears, and her team was up by 15 points. Katherine had played well, scoring 12 points and pulling down nine rebounds. She even had a couple of blocked shots that really stirred the crowd. "Why was Katherine upset?" Sammy wondered. She felt like she had to find out what was wrong. Neither Coach Williams nor the team was paying any attention to Katherine. As the game ended and the fans filtered out of the gym, Sammy noticed that the coaches were already in their offices making phone calls and reporting the score. This was one evening that Coach Williams had decided not to talk with the team.

Katherine was just about to leave when Sammy caught up to her. "Katherine, can we talk for a second?" she asked.

"Yeah, sure," Katherine replied.

Katherine and Sammy walked toward a vacant "cubbyhole" in the hallway, neither saying a word. "Are you all right?" Sammy asked.

"Yeah, I'm okay," Katherine said. After that response, Sammy realized that that was not the case.

"Nice try," Sammy said with a smile. All of a sudden, Katherine started to cry. Sammy was taken aback by Katherine's reaction, and she put her arm around her until she calmed down.

Finally Katherine said, "It's my Dad." Sammy really didn't know what she meant. She had only met Katherine's father a couple of times. He had seemed very quiet. She knew he was a track coach at another school, but that was about it.

When Katherine told Sammy that she had blown up at him the night before and told him she didn't want him at any more of her games, Sammy couldn't help but think of all of the games when he *had* been there. He hadn't said very much, but apparently there was no need to at the time. Katherine and her father seemed to have an understanding; all she had to do was perform perfectly, and everything would be fine. Over the span of the season, however, this apparently began to take its toll on Katherine.

During the past few games, Katherine had looked hesitant. She couldn't keep her eyes out of the stands, especially when she missed a shot or when the girl she was defending scored. Sammy noticed that Katherine's father hung his head in shame when this happened. If she was out of the game for even a breather or a drink of water, Katherine's eyes were focused on her father. He sat directly across from the bench in clear view. He would just stare her down with a disappointed look, often shaking his head in disgust.

As Katherine wiped the tears from her eyes, Sammy wondered why she, Coach Williams, and others on the team had not noticed something sooner. As she looked at Katherine, with her hands over her eyes and her head down, Sammy asked her what had happened that brought all of this about. "It's been going on for a while," she sobbed. "It's just been building up for so long."

"What's been going on?" Sammy asked, trying to conceal the urgency in her voice.

"He won't leave me alone," Katherine replied.

This response panicked Sammy. "What was Katherine talking about?" she thought. It seemed like an eternity before Katherine spoke up and broke the silence.

"It's bad enough playing a bad game, but then I have to go home and relive it. I am so sick of hearing how 'everyone else' would have played the game, especially him."

Katherine was letting herself go. She told Sammy that after every game, win or lose, when she got home, she and her father would "discuss" it. They would discuss how she had played, how her teammates had played, how her teammates hadn't gotten the ball to her enough, and how her coach did not know how to coach. She tried to stay away from him when she got home, if she even went home after the game (she usually tried to go to a friend's house for a few hours). But it was impossible to avoid him indefinitely. She felt like she was ready to crack from all the pressure. Between school, games, her dad, and trying to please everyone else, she was running herself ragged.

Sammy had thought Katherine was a dream player. She was so willing to work on her skills with Sammy, but it seemed as if Sammy was the only one to get along well with Katherine.

"I really don't get along too well with my teammates," Katherine had said many times before. "They don't like me very much. I guess they're jealous of me," she had told Sammy just two weeks ago. "You know, I do what I have to do to play ball," Katherine blurted out. "I may be too serious, but they're all a bunch of characters." Hearing this, Sammy realized for the first time that Katherine's personality did seem to clash with the others.

Katherine began to explain the conversation that had taken place the night before. "Dad tells me I need to be more of my own person and to do my own thing. 'Forget everyone else,' he says. So that is when I told him I didn't want him at any more of my games.

"It was really odd not having Dad here tonight," she said. "I thought that was what I wanted, but everything got so frustrating. I just blew up." He had at least done as she had asked, but it still wasn't helping. "I mean, we aren't even talking at home. We aren't even talking about the letters I'm receiving from colleges. It's so exciting, but I feel like I don't have anyone to share these events with. The excitement of games and the possibility of playing in college keep me motivated, but sometimes I really wonder if it's all worthwhile.

"I love basketball, and I really want to play in college," she said. "But I'm not having fun anymore. I certainly don't want to go to a college that's close to home; Dad wouldn't leave me alone.

"Basketball isn't my life like my father wants it to be," she said. "There are other things in my life that I care about, like school, but even my schoolwork is slipping. All I do is go home, get read the riot act, and go to my room and cry."

The whole discussion had made Sammy feel physically ill. She felt she had let Katherine down as a coach and as a friend. Sammy let out a long, heavy sigh.

Katherine continued, "My family is so divided about my basketball. Everyone in my house is getting sick of the bickering and complaining, especially me! Mom says she just wishes that Dad and I would settle this. My younger sister, Emily, swears she won't play basketball because of this." The pressures were just too great, Sammy thought.

To think that no one else on the coaching staff had even noticed any of Katherine's troubles began to confuse and upset Sammy . . . or had they noticed?

It was getting late, and it was time for Katherine and Sammy to go. Katherine knew that tonight there wouldn't be any talk of the game; there wouldn't be any talk at all. Her father hadn't been at the game to have anything to talk to her about.

The next morning, Sammy continued to be deeply concerned about what had happened. Sammy sees you walking past her office. With large searching eyes, she asks you if you've got the time to help her. After telling you the story, she asks, "What's the best way to handle this?

Question Guide

1. Describe the characters in this case.
   A. Sammy
   B. Katherine
   C. Coach Williams
   D. Katherine's father
   E. Katherine's teammates
2. Describe the main issues in this case.
3. As a sport psychology consultant, generate some courses of action that might assist Katherine.
4. How feasible is each course of action?
5. What are the ramifications for Katherine of each course of action?
6. As a sport psychology consultant, would you become involved in the relationship between Katherine and her father? Why or why not? Would you choose to involve Coach Williams? Why or why not?
7. How could you help Katherine lessen the pressure she feels from her father?
8. What could Katherine do differently?
9. What role does Sammy's relationship with Katherine play in this situation?

A Mile in Mufyrr's Shoes

Brian A. McGuire

THROUGH ITS CONNECTIONS with college recruiters and foreign Olympic runners, Western Military Academy (WMA) has taken in talented high school runners from numerous countries. This year was no exception. Another highly talented runner began his career as a WMA cadet.

When Mufyrr arrived, I was on an internship as a graduate assistant athletic trainer, working primarily with football players in the fall. I thus had only minor contact with the new star athlete during his cross-country season. Mufyrr came down to the training room very seldom. When he did, it was usually after a long run to treat minor tendonitis, and so the only information I knew about him was what I had heard others say.

It did not take me long to realize that Mufyrr's true specialty was track. At WMA, we are fortunate to have a new athletic center with an indoor track, allowing runners to train and compete year-round. Once football was over, I spent most of my time indoors. This allowed me to get to know Mufyrr as a person, and not just as a runner.

Everyone at the academy in one way or another knew Mufyrr. Because of his extreme talent, people either read about him in the *Cadet Chronicle* or heard about him from others. And because of the history of WMA's foreign stars, including three recent Olympians, Mufyrr was automatically placed in the same category. It seemed that everyone had high expectations for him and therefore followed his races.

When talking to Mufyrr and getting to know him, I realized that he seemed unaffected by his "Olympian-prospect" status. Many of the young cadets would surround Mufyrr and ask him, "Are you really going to the Olympics?" Mufyrr would simply smile and look down sheepishly, saying, "I don't know. That is two years away. I am going to train hard for them." To the younger cadets, Mufyrr's "working hard" was only a formality. Mufyrr had already qualified in their minds.

He was unassuming in every way. At 5'7" and 138 pounds, his slight physique was custom-built for middle-distance track events. His skin was a mocha color, and his jet black hair was kept short and parted down the middle. To handle himself as he had seemed remarkable to me. Mufyrr did not seem to understand pressure or expectations and showed no fear of not meeting those expectations. Mufyrr simply enjoyed his running, and whatever happened, happened. His training for the 800 meters was going very well, and he was winning every indoor meet that he entered. He was among the nation's ten fastest 400-meter runners, and he was also in the top ten for other races. As the indoor season was ending, Mufyrr was preparing to compete in the 800-meter run at the National Scholastic Indoor Championships, now only four days away. This was a big meet for Mufyrr because he could get national recognition by running well.

For most of the team, this was a transition period between indoor and outdoor track seasons, and so testing was being done on all track athletes for five different events: 800, 100, long jump, high jump, and shot put. This was merely "fun," and an attempt to give each athlete a combined-event score. The athletes merely added up their total points for all events and came up with their own all-around track-and-field scores.

I was in the training room that day when the "fun" competition was going on, the day that two other track athletes had to carry Mufyrr into the training room. Unable to walk, Mufyrr was moaning in agony as he neared my table.

Seeing Mufyrr in this way was a surreal experience. Here, the perfectly formed, perfectly adjusted athlete was damaged. I had never seen him when he wasn't anything except serene and under control.

"Mark, I felt my hamstring tear while doing the long jump," Mufyrr sputtered out.

I treated him immediately and again after dinner, which was before mandatory study hall. With the National Championships only four days away, his chances didn't look good for competing.

We performed three rehab sessions daily, but he was still unable to get back on the track, so his chances of winning a national championship were vanquished. To compound the problem, outdoor track was beginning, and with a pulled hamstring Mufyrr would not be able to train, let alone compete for possibly six to eight weeks. Then when he was ready to begin training, it would be at least two months before he was in peak shape again.

For the first few days, Mufyrr maintained his usual happy-go-lucky attitude. After one week of not being able to jog without pain, things seemed to change.

The injury had apparently devastated him. His sudden change caught me completely off guard.

"Come outside with me, Mufyrr. We need to talk," I instructed. Spending so much time with him lately, I had become very familiar with the pressure Mufyrr was feeling. It was 7:00 P.M. and nearly dark. We walked outside and sat down where we could be alone and where no one could see him "this way."

Mufyrr had been a member of the junior national soccer team in the United Arab Emirates when a track club recruited him two years ago. While in the track club, he was with many high-caliber, experienced international and Olympic runners and coaches. So, even though a little out of place in the track setting, Mufyrr matured quickly in this environment.

By the end of the season, he had already run five races under 1:52 in the 800 meters. He wanted to come to the United States for a good high school education in order to go to a top college. A college scholarship and getting a good education were foremost in his mind. "I know that I won't run forever, so I need to go to a good academic university for when I can no longer run." Mufyrr was fighting back tears now, and his words were very deliberate. Everything seemed to surface at that moment—all of the pressures he was under and, for the first time, questions about his ability.

Mufyrr was chosen to come to the United States before many other boys. He was told that if he could run under 1:54 in the 800 meters, his coach would arrange for him to go to the United States to school. The arrangements were made with WMA, but no other details were made available to him. Mufyrr's coach took care of all of the travel expenses and the arrangements to leave for the United States.

"I had to leave in the middle of the night very quickly because of the Gulf War. No one was allowed to leave the country. I never had a chance to say goodbye to my little brothers and sisters. I didn't want to see them cry when I told them I was leaving." Two silent tears slowly rolled down Mufyrr's cheeks. "I left with only my gym bag of clothes. They still look for me to come home every day. It was so very difficult for me to leave everyone, not knowing when I would see them again. I knew, though, that this might be my only chance, and so I knew I had to go."

Mufyrr had arrived in the United States not knowing anyone. He lives with the coach and his family at WMA. They have become his family for now. Hearing this young man's life story was tearing my heart out. His problems made mine seem so petty. How in the world could I help him? My greatest concerns were finishing my graduate degree in less than a year and keeping up the car payments on my '88 Escort. Heck, my entire family was one phone call away or a mere three-hour drive.

"Three boys from my country can now run 1:51," Mufyrr continued. "I talked to my high school coach yesterday. He wanted to know how the Nationals went for me. I told him that I pulled my hamstring and did not compete. Coach told me to make sure I got my leg 100 percent before running again."

That was somewhat of a relief to hear, however I still knew he was greatly affected by the injury. I sensed Mufyrr's feelings of despair and uncertainty.

"People here just don't understand. They do not *really* know me," he said.

It was then that you, a graduate student in sport psychology who would be receiving your Ph.D. soon, walked past the place we were sitting. I immediately recognized you and invited you to sit and hear this story.

Now Mufyrr and I are awaiting your response.

Question Guide

1. Describe the characters in this case
   A. Mufyrr
   B. The athletic trainer, who narrates the story
   C. The coach at WMA
   D. Mufyrr's family
2. Describe the main issues in this case. How would you prioritize the issues?
3. As a sport psychology consultant, generate some courses of action that might assist Mufyrr.
4. How feasible is each course of action?
5. What are the ramifications for Mufyrr of each course of action?
6. How do the expectations placed on Mufyrr affect him?
7. As a sport psychology consultant, what would you do to help Mufyrr deal with the injury and the pressure that the injury is causing?
8. Would you handle this case on your own, or would you consider additional assistance? If so, what type of help, and whom would you contact?

7

COMPOSURE
AND EMOTIONAL
CONTROL

Rotella's Insights and Observations

Great athletes learn to use and express emotions that facilitate performance, and they learn to tone down and control the expression of emotions that hinder performance. Losing control of harmful emotions and panic are deadly to effective performance under pressure. Developing composure requires honest self-awareness, mental discipline, emotional resilience, and the willingness to take personal responsibility for one's actions.

His Own Enemy

Bill Allyson

THE FALL SEASON WAS going well for the golf team as far as wins and losses were concerned. At 3–0 with three matches remaining, Southern Michigan University was already making a stronger run than most teams from the South, with longer outdoor season. The weakness in this success, however, was that one of the team's five players did not contribute a single score to the winning totals in the first three matches.

Since I had worked successfully with some of the golfers, Coach Knox suggested to Zac, the player who had not yet contributed, that he see me. Later that day, Coach Knox called me.

"Do you know Zac?" he asked. Before I could answer, he continued. "Well, he's got all the skills in every part of his game. He hits fine off the tee, plays his irons better than anyone on the team, has a strong short game, and can putt. But he's not scoring for us at all. Nothing. Zero. And because he doesn't, and the rest of the team knows they can't count on him, it puts pressure on the other guys. He's one of our best golfers, but he's not helping us one bit."

The fact that Zac wasn't helping the scores was one concern of Coach's, but he also showed his concern for how the team and Zac were getting along and enjoying golf. "Last year, as a freshman, Zac had some great rounds, scored for us, and was a nice addition to the team. This year, though, after not scoring for us in the first two tournaments, he started avoiding the other guys, and I'm not sure they didn't start avoiding him too."

Coach went on to tell me about Zac's summer, which included qualifying for the Western Amateur and the U.S. Amateur tournaments. A few years before that, when Zac was in high school, he was the state runner-up twice, a U.S. Junior Amateur qualifier, and Seattle All-City Junior Champion.

"He hits so many sweet shots that it's sad he has a couple of short lapses each round that add four to six and even eight strokes to his score. If it weren't for that, he'd be a medalist."

Just then my other line rang, and I put Coach on hold. The other caller was Zac. I switched back to Coach Knox and told him I had to go but that I'd stop by and see him within the next few days. Then I got back to Zac.

After introducing himself and explaining how he had heard of me, Zac began telling me that he plays excellent golf and just doesn't know why he doesn't score better. "I have a few spots during most rounds where I hit a completely stupid shot, but so does everyone else. Yet I don't score like everyone else on my team. I don't get it." After a short pause, Zac continued. "You know, it really makes me mad when I hit those two or three stupid shots each round. I just can't believe I do that, when I'll have identical shots, and maybe even three or four identical shots to the ones I screw up, and I'll hit them stiff. But when I hit the lousy ones, that really throws me off. As if it weren't bad enough me sculling a chip, or hitting my five iron into the pond or out of bounds, I feel so mad and I have to work so hard to get it back that I usually put too much on the next couple of shots.

"Another thing I do is I find myself thinking about the score and how I don't have a chance to break par unless I have a super hole. Then I'm under the gun, and if I screw up again, well it really gets me steamed, and my chances of doing well really go down the drain.

"Do you think you can help me?" he asked.

"I'd be glad to work with you, Zac. And yes, I believe you can improve your game. Do you want to talk now, or would you like to set up a time to meet and discuss this?"

"If we could meet tomorrow at 11 o'clock in the morning, that would be best for me," Zac replied. "Can I come to your office then?"

"Yes, that will work. I'll see you then, Zac."

Without setting the phone down, I dialed Coach's number to see if he was still in his office. Fortunately, I reached him. "Coach, sorry I had to cut our conversation, but I was thinking about those lapses you said Zac has. Can you tell me more about them?"

Coach Knox and I talked for about 20 minutes. He told me how, out of nowhere and without warning, Zac would hit an uncharacteristically errant shot that would usually cost him a stroke or two. Then for the next two or three shots, or even two or three holes, Zac would hang his head, not talk to the others, and generally sulk. In addition, he would slam his bag down and would forcefully hit his club against the ground when another shot didn't go exactly as planned. According to Coach, Zac seemed to be a nasty storm picking up steam. Then all of a sudden, he would go back to hitting sweet shots, walking with his head up, and talking to the others in his group. Coach Knox even went as far as to call Zac a "Dr. Jekyll and Mr. Hyde" case.

Coach said, "I truly wish he could consistently play like he does most of his round. He would take this team from being ranked 12th in the nation to national champs if we could count on him to do that. I mean it. Even this year, I bet we could contend for the National Championship if Zac held it together for a couple of rounds rather than a couple of holes at a time. What do you think we can do with him?"

"You told him to call me, right? Well, I'll talk with him and see how he can score better and contribute more to the success of the team," I said. "Thanks for all of your help, Coach." That ended my talk with Coach Knox. But I know Zac is coming in tomorrow morning, and he'll be getting ready to go back on the road in five days to compete again. I need to keep all of this in mind and be ready when he gets here.

Question Guide

1. Describe the characters in this case.
   A. Zac
   B. Coach Knox
2. Describe the main issues in this case.
3. What are some possible reasons for Zac's loss of control, erratic behavior, and poor performance on the golf course?
4. As a sport psychology consultant, generate some courses of action that might assist Zac.
5. How feasible is each course of action?
6. What are the ramifications for Zac of each course of action?
7. As a sport psychology consultant, would you involve Coach Knox in your discussions with Zac? Why or why not?
8. Are there deeper issues? Would you handle this case on your own, or would you consider additional assistance? If so, state the specific type of help you would seek, whom you would contact, and how you would help Zac get this additional assistance.

Break Point: A Player's Anger
and a Coach's Decision

David A. Striegel

"I can't believe this! I shouldn't even be out here," shouted Mark, Hutchinson State's number two player and co-captain of the men's tennis team. Down 0–2, love–15 in the second set of his match against Faulkner College, Mark was beginning to erupt. He had been boiling since the middle of the first set. After slicing another return of serve into the net, Mark stalked away from the baseline and screamed, "How many points are you going to give him?! No wonder you're getting stomped!"

He slammed the head of his racket into the fence behind the court and looked upward in disgust, hoping the match would end any minute. His eyes inadvertently met those of his girlfriend, Kathy, who was seated among a small group of fans in the bleachers. Mark quickly turned away, not wanting to see the expression on Kathy's face in reaction to his most recent outburst. Mark noted that Kathy was trying her best to focus on the players on the court while some fans seated behind her made derogatory comments about his behavior.

An interesting pair, Kathy and Mark had been dating for almost two years. Kathy was nearly a straight-A student who studied for at least a couple of hours every day, while Mark was barely a B student who would much rather be playing tennis than studying. Lately, though, he had focused more on his studies. He just couldn't stop worrying about his senior thesis. It was due in a little over a month, and he had barely begun the research.

The score of the match was love–30, and his opponent seemed to be playing with a great deal of confidence. As a first serve went flying by him, Mark quickly moved to the ad-court as if anxious to end the match. "Forget it! This is ridiculous. You played better than this in seventh grade!"

Mark went on to lose the match, seemingly giving up, or "tanking," after falling behind 0–3 in the second set. His match lasted a little over one hour and punctuated an already lousy day. Unfortunately, this day seemed no different from any other in the past three weeks. Slamming the gate to the court as he left, Mark shouted, "I hate this!" He knew everyone watching could hear him, but he did not care.

Nineteen eighty-two was the last year the men's tennis team had a winning season. Even then, their record barely reached .500 at 10–9. Interestingly, HSU was a school with a solid athletic department, overall, to accompany a tremendous academic reputation. Though the tennis program received little financial support other than the obligatory budget required to function at the Division I level, expectations for success were traditionally high. Those on the outside looking in routinely remarked that they couldn't understand how HSU avoided having a successful tennis program. Being located in the Florida Panhandle carried with it certain disadvantages. Many people assumed that every school in Florida played great tennis. However, without similar facilities and resources, HSU couldn't compete year in and year out with the top 20 schools in the state. Though the team had shown steady improvement over the past couple of years, HSU had not been ranked in the NCAA top 50 since 1980.

Now the team was being led by first-year coach Jeff Hanrahan. As the lone assistant coach for the past three years, Coach Hanrahan was perceived by the team as knowing his players well. He was more of a friend to them than most coaches were to their players. Hanrahan's first year as a head coach had been difficult, yet exciting. Hanrahan treated the team as a group of intelligent, high-achieving kids who had yet to come together as a cohesive unit. Mark knew that it had been frustrating for Coach to watch them struggle to compete with very average Division I teams for the past three years. Coach Hanrahan was convinced that the kids could be competitive with almost anyone if they were taught more about the mental side of the game, including how to function as a team in an individual sport. Having earned a master's degree in sport psychology, Coach Hanrahan taught his team about cohesion. However, he wasn't sure how to handle Mark's outbursts and erratic play.

An outstanding doubles and a solid singles player, Mark had a successful junior season, posting a 13–5 record with his partner, Sean, at number two doubles, and a 10–8 record at number four singles. Expectations were high entering this season as Mark moved up in both singles and doubles. In addition, he and Sean, who played number one singles, were voted cocaptains for the upcoming season.

Mark and Sean had been best friends since they met on the HSU campus three and a half years ago. That they were friends at all was somewhat of a surprise.

Having grown up in South Carolina and Georgia, respectively, they competed against one another in a number of regional junior tournaments. They became bitter rivals, often meeting in the semifinals or finals of tournaments. Sean beat Mark nine of eleven times they met, but the matches were always close. The rivalry developed from the competition and the bitterness from their parents. Both sets of parents were very involved in their sons' tennis and looked at their tennis careers as a means of financial security. As a result, each time Mark and Sean played, their parents would bad-mouth each other in the days leading up to the match. However, when the two boys finally had the opportunity to hang out by themselves, they realized they had a great deal in common. Thus, their friendship was born.

Two team matches remain in what began as the breakthrough season for HSU. The team bolted to a 10–0 start, beating three teams ranked in the NCAA top 75. However, since then they have lost seven of their last eight matches, with two top 20 teams left to play. During this slide, all the players have stayed hungry to win, with the exception of Mark.

Mark and Sean combined to lead the team to their best start in school history. Mark was playing particularly well, with singles and doubles records of 8–2 and 9–1, respectively. However, midway through the season he started losing singles matches by larger and larger margins, culminating in a 6–2, 6–0 loss in his most recent match to an opponent he defeated easily last year. On the same day, he and Sean were upset at number one doubles in a close team loss to a conference rival. Though not solely responsible for the team's defeat, Mark's losses only served to magnify his continuing struggles. The feeling among his teammates had reached the point that they expected Mark to lose his singles match, which meant the team was behind before the first ball was played.

The next match was against the last-place team in the conference. Mark knew that Coach Hanrahan viewed it as an opportunity for the team, and especially Mark, to play without the pressure they normally felt when playing tougher opponents. This might allow them to have fun and win, he thought, something they hadn't done for some time. However, Mark did not want to make this trip, and he set up a meeting with Coach Hanrahan in the coach's office. Hanrahan was blindsided by the request.

"Coach, I don't think I can make the trip to Augusta. My back is killing me."

"Your back still hurts? What happened?" asked the coach.

"I don't know, I guess I hurt it against Faulkner yesterday."

"Have you gone to see the trainer yet?"

"No, not yet. I'm on my way now."

"Let me know what she says. I can't imagine you not being ready by Monday," the coach said.

After a visit to the training room, Mark reported that his back was still bothering him the day before the match. Though not happy about it, Coach Hanrahan noted that "Mark may need a little time off." Coach obliged and allowed him to stay home to receive treatment in the training room and catch up on his schoolwork. Meanwhile, the team embarked on their trip to Augusta, hoping to regain their confidence.

The team won easily without Mark. The sole freshman on the squad moved into Mark's number two singles and number one doubles spots and played great. The feeling of the team was one of elation combined with relief. They had finally broken out of their slump. Coach Hanrahan seemed encouraged and happy to see the kids smile and laugh again. However, Mark knew that coach's happiness was tempered by his concern for him.

Mark wondered if Coach Hanrahan would check up on him with Sherry, the team athletic trainer. The next day, Coach Hanrahan asked Sherry how long Mark might be out of action. Much to the coach's chagrin, she replied that Mark had pulled a muscle in his lower back but that it shouldn't be enough to keep him from playing. She said she thought Mark didn't go on the trip to Augusta because of his being behind in his schoolwork. Coach Hanrahan thanked her for the information and went back to his office upstairs. This was the first he had heard of this. He had always tried to keep on top of how his team was doing in school, but somehow Mark slipped by. He was not particularly surprised that Mark had fallen behind. He typically put tennis ahead of school anyway. Given this tendency, it did not make sense that school would affect his performance so dramatically. There had to be something else.

Coach Hanrahan had talked to Mark on a number of occasions about trouble he was having on the court, particularly his outbursts of anger. But Mark thought his outbursts were justified. He would say, "The courts were too slow," or "The wind was blowing too hard." Mark believed that his problems came from external sources that, in his mind, he couldn't control. *He* was never at fault.

Mark had always been a formidable doubles player. In fact, he and Sean could break into the NCAA top 30 with a win against one of their two remaining opponents. When playing with Sean, he seemed more focused and emotionally composed than when playing singles. At worst, he would let out an occasional shout of motivation, like "Come on!" but rarely anything negative. Yet when he played singles, his temper seemed to get the best of him. Often, if he didn't play well in the first few games of a match, he worked himself into such a frenzy that he seemed no longer to care if he won or lost. This season he had received three point penalties for poor behavior, either for shouting or throwing his racket.

Mark knew that his friends couldn't understand why he got so angry when he was normally very laid-back. Last year it seemed as though he was comfortable and relaxed on the court. Now he seemed to struggle just to keep from losing it every time he played by himself.

There is an outside chance that HSU could receive an invitation to the NCAA Men's Tennis Championships. However, they must play well against both of their remaining opponents and in their conference tournament. Mark knows that if he plays well, the team has a legitimate shot at making the NCAA tournament field. But if he plays the way he has over the last few weeks, the team has virtually no chance.

Coach Hanrahan has approached you, a first-year professor at HSU specializing in sport psychology, with this situation. Where do you start?

Question Guide

1. Describe the characters in this case.
   A. Mark
   B. Coach Hanrahan
   C. Mark's and Sean's parents
   D. Sean and Mark's other teammates
   E. Sherry, the athletic trainer
2. Describe the main issues in this case.
3. What are some possible reasons for Mark's outbursts, erratic behavior, and poor performance?
4. As a sport psychology consultant, generate some courses of action that might assist Mark.
5. How feasible is each course of action?
6. What are the ramifications for Mark of each course of action?
7. How do the expectations placed on Mark affect him?
8. As a sport psychology consultant, would you involve Coach Hanrahan in your discussions with Mark? Why or why not?
9. How would you help Mark deal with the match's outcome?
10. Would you handle this case on your own, or would you consider additional assistance? If so, what type of help, and whom would you contact?

8

PSYCHOLOGICAL
REHABILITATION

Rotella's Insights and Observations

Injury is a necessary risk inherent in training and conditioning in sport. Part of becoming a champion athlete is the attitude one takes toward psychological rehabilitation when injured. Responding to the motivation of training-room personnel and inspiring them, as well as oneself, is necessary. But it is also important to develop the toughness to play with and through pain and to know when to give in to pain and get rest and receive treatment. These latter skills should be considered equally important.

Ted's Turmoil

Thomas Johnston

TED JACKSON IS THE ONLY senior who plays basketball for Major University, a predominantly white school. He is a lean six-foot-tall African-American. Ted was a high school All-American from Philadelphia's inner city, where he was the star of his team, averaging over 30 points and almost seven assists per game during his high school career.

Ted's first two years in college were very frustrating. He did not play much as a freshman or sophomore, averaging just under five minutes per game. However, this was not totally unexpected, as Major University had a reputation for point guards who went on to excel in the professional leagues. It had always been Ted's dream to play for Major University and then play professional basketball. His parents had both attended Major University and had met there as incoming freshmen. They were delighted when Ted chose Major.

As a junior, Ted became the starting point guard. For the first ten games, he averaged 14 points and 6.5 assists per game. He was the consummate point guard, directing traffic and, in his coach's words, "coaching the team on the court." Ted's accomplishments did not go unnoticed by the media, either. One article in the local paper said, "Jackson is a sure bet to make the pros. He is just another in a long line of point guards from Major University to display such great leadership qualities." Three days after this article appeared, Ted suffered a season-ending injury. When he drove the lane, he was undercut by his defender and landed on his side. Ted's first thought was that his basketball career was over. Although he could leave the court under his own power, Ted knew his knee and back were severely injured. The result of the fall was a herniated disk and stretched ligaments in his right knee.

After the game, Ted called his parents and told them what had happened. He told them that he was going to see the doctor the next day. He also told them that the trainer thought he had probably just bruised his back, but that he might have a serious knee injury. Ted was scared, and it must have showed because his mother started crying on the phone. His father told him that he would have to make his body stronger and that this was going to be the biggest challenge of his athletic career.

When Ted went to the doctors, he was advised that he had several choices. They could operate on both his back and knee. He could have one or the other operated on, or he could go through an extensive rehabilitation program. The one thing the doctors were positive about was that Ted's season was over. This was extremely disappointing for Ted. He had never suffered an injury in his life except for a couple of minor sprained ankles. Those injuries had never stopped him from playing in a game, much less caused him to miss a season.

After his appointment with the doctors, Ted talked to the coach, who told him that he would not lose his starting position as point guard and that he was counting on Ted to lead the team on and off the court in his senior season. However, Coach also told him that his starting position depended upon how intensely he rehabilitated his injuries. The coach planned to check with the training staff to see how Ted was responding to treatment. This did not worry Ted because he was determined to recover from his injuries and be in the best possible shape. During their meeting, Ted felt that Coach really cared about him, but after the meeting he realized that Coach never asked him how he was doing. He seemed more concerned that Ted was going to rehabilitate his injuries so he would be ready to play next season.

To rehabilitate his back, Ted was advised that he would have to go to therapy two hours a day, four days per week. Ted's initial reaction was that this was going to be the biggest challenge of his life. However, he knew that once the rehab was over he would be very proud of himself. He also knew that this was his only chance of becoming the starting point guard and being a professional basketball player. Ted believed that his injury may have been a blessing in disguise because he felt that his overall strength would increase from his rehab program. Coach also told him that his injury may help him become a smarter basketball player because he would have the opportunity to watch games from a different perspective.

When pickup games started this fall, Ted felt that he was ready to play. Although he is still a little rusty, his knee feels stronger than ever. Ted believes that even though he missed most of the previous season, he is seeing the court better than before. The only aspect of his game that he feels is missing is his ability to drive to the basket and then either take the shot or dish off. Logically he knows that his knee can take the punishment, but he has not been able to get up the nerve to drive with the same reckless abandon that was so successful for him in the first ten games of his junior season.

The failure to drive aggressively is starting to become a problem for Ted because he has noticed that this is the major strength of the player who replaced him last year. In addition, there is a first-year player who can also drive to the basket quite effectively. Although Coach guaranteed him his old starting position, Ted is beginning to doubt that he can do the job. He also wonders if he can still trust the coach. He remembers what Coach told him, but he can remember several times in the past that Coach said one thing and did another. Ted comes to you. How do you help him?

Question Guide

1. Describe the characters in this case.
   A. Ted
   B. Ted's coach
   C. Ted's parents
2. Describe the main issues in this case. How would you prioritize the issues?
3. What are some possible reasons for Ted's loss of confidence and the less aggressive play that results?
4. As a sport psychology consultant, generate some courses of action that might assist Ted.
5. How feasible is each course of action?
6. What are the ramifications for Ted of each course of action?
7. As a sport psychology consultant, would you involve Ted's coach in your discussions with Ted? Why or why not?
8. How would you help Ted deal with the season's outcome (starter or non-starter)?
9. Are there deeper issues related to Ted's injury? Would you handle this case on your own, or would you consider additional assistance? If so, what type of help, and whom would you contact?

The Untimely Collision

Kathryn C. Wilder

 SARA WAS THE NUMBER ONE soccer recruit at Ivy University, and she was also highly recruited by many other Division I schools. She chose Ivy not only because of its strong soccer program, but for its academic reputation. Ivy University's soccer coach, Robin Locke, began to recruit Sara heavily during her junior year of high school. Coach Locke had been the head coach at Ivy University for three years, and she was intent on creating a winning program.

Coach Locke was 28 years old and had been a highly competitive college soccer player at a Division I school. She was so zealous in her recruitment of Sara that she even visited her guidance counselor on multiple occasions. As a further enticement, Coach Locke persuaded Sara to attend a U.S. development soccer camp hosted by Ivy University. At age 17, Sara was invited to attend a national-level soccer camp, placing her one step away from the national team.

Sara was a talented and well-disciplined team player. Coach Locke recognized her as the cornerstone around which to build a winning team, and she relayed her high expectations to Sara. Sara was so flattered by Coach Locke's promises about the program and her role on the team that she chose to attend Ivy.

During Sara's first year at Ivy, she received a great deal of positive feedback about her performance. That season, she was the only freshman to start every game. In high school she played halfback, but Coach Locke moved her to forward, which afforded Sara greater scoring opportunities. In the championship game, Sara scored the winning goal in sudden-death double overtime.

During the summer, Coach Locke asked Sara and two of her teammates to teach at regional soccer camps. Sara enjoyed teaching younger players soccer skills, and she retained a good player-coach relationship with Coach Locke. As a sophomore, Sara began to recognize an undercurrent of pessimism in Coach Locke. The coach had a tendency to give up on her team or players if she sensed that there was a chance of losing the game. She was volatile on the side-lines with the team, and her words of criticism stung not only an individual player's abilities but her personality as well. Sara also viewed Coach Locke's position assignments as unpredictable. Overall, Sara recognized that Coach Locke's coaching strategy could have been more effective.

Sara never questioned Coach Locke at practice, but her respect for her diminished with every haphazard outburst. She began to take more of a leadership role on the field toward the end of her sophomore year and was seen as a versatile all-around player by her teammates. Sara was the second leading scorer on the team and was the fastest player on the squad.

During the spring of Sara's sophomore year, she organized a triathlon team at Ivy University. In her triathlon debut, she qualified for the collegiate National Championships to be held in September of her junior year. Sara immediately contacted Coach Locke and asked her permission to attend Nationals even though it interrupted their preseason practice schedule. Coach Locke was excited that one of her athletes had qualified for Nationals. However, she was apprehensive about Sara's participation and questioned her commitment to the soccer team.

The summer before Sara's junior year, she competed in several triathlons and consistently placed in the top in her age group. She also played in a regional soccer league and taught soccer at one of Coach Locke's camps. As a result, Sara was in top condition at the beginning of preseason. She had two weeks of preseason training for soccer that overlapped with her triathlon training. One week into preseason, Coach Locke gave her players a day off from soccer. Sara took advantage of the opportunity to go for a short training ride on her bicycle.

Sara rode her bicycle on a well-traveled divided highway before reaching rural roads. She was riding along at 20 to 25 mph when she was struck by a driver who didn't see her. Too late to apply her brakes, Sara was hurled through the air and slid across the pavement. Fortunately, Sara was wearing a helmet, but she was still knocked unconscious when her head crashed into a stone wall.

Sara regained consciousness just before being taken by ambulance to the hospital. After rigorous tests, it was determined that Sara had no major injuries, although she did sustain multiple abrasions, a severely bruised shoulder, and a potential knee injury. Ivy's sport medicine staff recommended that Sara take at least three weeks off from playing to fully recover from her injury.

Coach Locke was not as patient as the rehabilitation staff and frequently asked Sara if she was ready to return to play. Sara was also anxious to return to the playing field. She felt that Coach Locke would resent her if she didn't have a speedy recovery. She even began to wonder if she shared the blame for the injury.

Perhaps she shouldn't have been preparing for a triathlon during soccer season. She forced a premature recovery and was back on the playing field within six days of the accident.

Upon her return, Coach Locke criticized Sara when she was unable to execute moves at full speed. Although she was still sore from the accident, Sara felt determined to show Coach Locke that nothing could stop her. Sara's outlook changed from having fun to proving herself, but pressing to prove herself hindered her natural style and finesse. Furthermore, Sara wondered about Coach Locke's motives for rushing her return and whether the coach had even considered her psychological readiness to return to play.

During her junior year, Sara played less consistently, and the team had a mediocre season. Coach Locke removed Sara early from a few games, even when Ivy University was losing. In her postseason meeting with the coach, Sara attributed her difficult season to a bad start. She was afraid that Coach Locke would not respond well to her insinuation that an early return had been forced, therefore she did not broach the topic. Sara was also unsure of how to address the issue of being criticized by Coach Locke.

Both Sara and her coach had been looking forward to Sara's senior year, in which she was elected captain of the team. She had a hat trick in the season opener. The team was young, so she felt her leadership role was very important. She felt comfortable and natural as the person to represent her team. Unfortunately, the team lost the following four games. Coach Locke became highly critical of Sara and the other four seniors on the team. She blamed them for the team's losses, became desperate for a win, and began pulling up junior varsity players to varsity. She didn't start Sara on a number of occasions, and she sharply curtailed her playing time. Sara had never sat on the bench for more than 15 minutes, and as team captain it was an awkward position for her.

Sara has come to you, Ivy University's sport psychology consultant, wondering about Coach Locke's player selection and commitment to winning this year. She also wants to know what she and the other seniors can do to improve the performance and success of the team during the last half of their senior season.

Question Guide

1. Describe the characters in this case
   A. Sara
   B. Coach Robin Locke
2. Describe the main issues in this case. How would you prioritize the issues?
3. What are some possible reasons for Coach Locke's loss of confidence in Sara? Are these reasons justified?
4. As a sport psychology consultant, generate some courses of action that might assist Sara.
5. How feasible is each course of action?
6. What are the ramifications for Sara of each course of action?
7. As a sport psychology consultant, would you involve Coach Locke in your discussions with Sara? Why or why not?
8. How would you help Sara deal with the season's outcome (starter or non-starter, win or lose)?
9. Describe any areas of conflict in the coach-player relationship.
10. Would you handle this case on your own, or would you consider additional assistance? If so, what type of help, and whom would you contact?

9

DEDICATION AND
COMMITMENT

Rotella's Insights
and Observations

There is no question that in today's world of sport, prioritizing time and energy for sport is a minimal requirement. Athletes must be willing to commit themselves and sustain that commitment for a prolonged period. Simply talking about commitment or being committed some of the time or when in the mood will not suffice. In developing this level of dedication, athletes must take care not to take sport so seriously that their self-image and self-esteem become totally dependent on performance results and they lose perspective on life. Keeping perspective is a delicate balancing act.

The Tormented Transfer Student

Thomas Johnston

Bobby's dream is to play on an NCAA Division I tennis team. He did not receive any Division I scholarship offers after high school, so when he went to Scholar College, he had to participate in the walk-on tournament. The coach told all the walk-ons that the winner of the tournament would make the team as the number 12 man on the team. For two consecutive years Bobby tried out for the tennis team, and for two consecutive years he lost in the last match and failed to make the team.

A small, thin boy of about five and a half feet, Bobby does not look the part of a big-time tennis player. However, his game is very explosive, and he is able to generate tremendous power on his ground strokes and return of serve. Opponents in the juniors were usually bigger than Bobby and often thought they would have an easy match because of his size. They were often mistaken. As a junior tennis player Bobby did well, but not great. He won his high school conference tennis championships and was ranked number 11 in his state. He did not attain a national junior ranking because only the top eight players from his state qualified for the national junior tennis tournaments. Probably because of his size and lack of a national junior ranking, Bobby did not receive scholarship offers to any Division I schools. Several small colleges contacted Bobby, expressing interest in him as a tennis player, and some even offered him a scholarship. Bobby, however, wanted to play at the Division I level.

During his second year at Scholar, he decided to transfer to Major University. Although his primary reason for transferring schools was to fulfill his dream of playing Division I tennis, he also wanted to attend a school with an equally outstanding academic reputation. In addition, Bobby was having trouble establishing and maintaining relationships. He perceived that a new start at a new school would solve his problems. Bobby's parents encouraged his decision to transfer because it brought him closer to home.

When fall arrived, Bobby went to the tennis coach and signed up for the walk-on tennis tournament. Coach Donnelly was then in his first year as head coach at Major University after serving as the assistant coach for the three previous years. He had also played for Major ten years ago. Coach Warner, who was in his first year of coaching, was also a former college player. Coaches Donnelly and Warner were happy to have an open tryout because they thought that they might find a "diamond in the rough." The tournament would be double elimination, and the top player would make the team.

All that week, Bobby practiced with the other guys trying out for the team. He never spoke to the guys about his experiences at Scholar, but he did use these memories to motivate himself in his practices. During these practice sessions, Bobby felt that he was hitting the ball great. His arm was beginning to feel a little sore when he hit serves, but otherwise he felt strong, physically and mentally. Watching his fellow competitors, he knew that he had a great chance of making the team.

Thursday night, Bobby barely slept because he was so nervous. By the time his match started Friday afternoon, he was exhausted. The player Bobby was matched up against was also a transfer. However, Bobby was relieved because he had played him a set in practice the previous week and had beaten him by the score of 6–2. Today's match, however, was a disaster. The first set was over in 30 minutes. By the time Bobby got his game going, he was down 5–1. He lost the set 6–2 and went on to lose the match 6–2, 6–3. If Bobby was to make the team now, he would have to win the remaining four matches.

Friday night, Bobby went to a party because he thought he had little or no chance to make the team. Normally he stayed home because he wanted to make sure he got his rest. The following day, Bobby played great. He won both of his matches in straight sets. The first match was a hard-fought contest that he won 7–5, 6–4. Although the scores did not reflect it, the second match was also closely contested. He won this one 6–3, 6–2. Bobby was beginning to think he had a good chance. He had seen the last three remaining players during the previous week's practice and felt that if he played up to his ability, he could win.

Saturday night, Bobby stayed at home. He watched television and thought about his upcoming matches. Sunday morning came, and Bobby was eager to play. He had a good warm-up, and his arm felt strong and loose. The first match was a nail-biter. Bobby won the first set 7–5. He was down 5–3 before raising the level of his game. He won the last four games of that first set and the first three games of the second. At this point, his opponent began to hit the ball as hard as he could. It seemed like he had given up, but to Bobby's dismay the balls went in. With renewed hope his opponent battled back to a tiebreaker. Bobby lost the breaker 8–6, and now a third set would have to be played. Bobby started strong again and got the early break. This time his opponent could not break back, and Bobby won the final set 6–4. That afternoon, Bobby would play the final match to make the team.

After a small lunch, Bobby went back to his room to shower and get ready for his match. He tried to take a nap but could not stop thinking about what lay ahead. He also could not help thinking that he was in the same position at Scholar. Thinking back, he knew he had choked those matches. He wondered if he would choke again. Finally he decided to listen to some music and stretch. At 3:30 he walked out to the tennis courts for his 4:00 match. When he got there Coach Donnelly was talking with John, his opponent. Bobby wondered what they were talking about. The coach wished both players well and gave them a can of balls for their match.

Like most of Bobby's matches, this one was hard-fought and full of exciting points. Neither player could establish any momentum, and the first set ended on a miss-hit forehand winner in John's favor. The second set was not as close. John let down after winning such a close first set, and Bobby was able to get the early break. He served out the set, winning it 6–3. Bobby continued to hold on to the momentum, gaining an early break and holding on to it until he reached 5–3 in the third set. Serving at 5–3, Bobby reminded himself to play one point at a time. He won the first three points of the game and had triple match point. At this juncture Bobby lost it. He was sure he had the match won. Unfortunately the match was not over. Bobby made a couple of mistakes, and John came back to win that game and hold his serve to tie the match 5–5. John won the next two games easily and went on to win the match 7–5 in the third set.

After Coach Donnelly congratulated John, Bobby looked up at the coach hoping to hear that he was going to be on the team anyway. He thought he deserved to be because the match was so close. Before Coach Donnelly could say anything, Bobby told him that he would do anything to be on the team and that the reason he had transferred to Major was to play on the tennis team. Coach told him that because the match was so close, he would think about it and give him a call with an answer by Wednesday. On Thursday Bobby had heard nothing from the coach. He called him Thursday night, and the coach said that he was sorry but that he could not be on the team.

No one on the team saw Bobby for the rest of the fall and most of the spring season. At the end of the school year, Coach Warner saw Bobby and asked him how things were going. Bobby said fine and told the assistant coach that he was planning on trying out for the team next year. Bobby asked him not to say anything to Coach Donnelly. That afternoon Coach Warner simply mentioned to Coach Donnelly that he had seen Bobby. Without any prompting, the head coach said, "I hope he doesn't plan on trying out for the team because there is no way I'm going to let him even try out, much less play. He's way too unstable. Who would transfer schools just to play tennis? Maybe if you had a scholarship, but no one in their right mind would transfer if they didn't already have a spot on the team."

Realizing that he had made a mistake by telling the head coach about seeing Bobby, Coach Warner began to feel overwhelmed and inexperienced. That evening he calls you, a sport psychology consultant who is familiar with the tennis team's coaches and players. "Now I'm in the middle of this awkward situations," he said. "Bobby trusts me and is looking forward to making the team next year. He still has two years of eligibility remaining. I believe he could help us as a leader off the court because I'm not sure how much he'll play. But right now, I don't know what to do about how much Bobby wants to be on the team and how much Coach Donnelly doesn't want anything to do with him. What can I do?"

Question Guide

1. Describe the characters in this case.
   A. Bobby
   B. Coach Donnelly
   C. Coach Warner
2. Describe the main issues in this case. How would you prioritize the issues?
3. What are some possible reasons for Bobby's lack of performance on the tennis court?
4. As a sport psychology consultant, generate some courses of action that might assist Bobby.
5. How feasible is each course of action?
6. What are the ramifications for Bobby of each course of action?
7. As a sport psychology consultant, would you involve Coach Donnelly or Coach Warner in your discussions with Bobby? Why or why not?
8. How would you help Coach Warner deal with Coach Donnelly regarding Bobby's desire to be on the tennis team next season?
9. Describe any areas of conflict in the coach-player relationship.
10. How does Coach Donnelly's perception of Bobby affect the coach's decision to not let Bobby try out for the team next season?

Just Go Play

Jana L. Maas

"I CAN'T BELIEVE Lisa and I are such good friends. It just seems so ironic," Sonny blurted out as I greeted her in the hallway. As we walked together toward the gym, she told me she often thought to herself how odd it was that things between her and Lisa had worked out the way they had.

Sonny smiled as she thought about the first time the two had met. As she walked into the first day of preseason two years ago, with the shiny parquet floor, the bright lights, and the empty bleachers, Lisa and the veterans were lined up, ready to show the rookies the ropes.

At first, their personalities clashed. Lisa, a senior starter, was easygoing and didn't seem to get too worked up about school or what other people thought of her. Sonny, a junior and Lisa's backup, worked feverishly on her schoolwork and lived and died by what other people thought of her. They each had their own shining moments, though. Sonny's were in the classroom, and Lisa's were on the court. Strangely, what would usually seem to tear teammates apart somehow made their friendship more meaningful.

On the basketball court, Lisa led a charmed life. She had "soft" hands and was a gifted shooter. In contrast, Sonny had a difficult time on the court. As hard as Sonny would practice, coming early and staying late, her playing time never increased. "I have to always give 110 percent," she would say. "I will get my chance, and I'm going to be ready. Plus my team needs me to push them." Sonny was mostly a practice player and had to play against Lisa as well as learn Lisa's position since she was her substitute.

"I appreciate how much you make me work at practice," Lisa would tell Sonny. "You deserve so much; you don't get credit for how valuable you are."

That made Sonny feel better, but sometimes when it came to game time, Sonny got quietly frustrated. When she did get playing time and someone would say, "You played well tonight," Sonny would politely say thank you but deny it to herself.

Sonny's playing time, or lack thereof, was really bothering her this year. She decided to set up a meeting with her coach. Coach Blair was a young coach. He was very good at his job, but he lacked years of experience at the Division II level. He was a great communicator and very positive with the girls. He wanted everyone to enjoy their basketball careers. His relaxed style made him comfortable to be around, easy to talk to, and a fun guy. He made practices fun, but the girls still had to work hard. Given his upbeat personality, the girls didn't mind the hard practices.

"I understand I'm not the best player on the team, Coach," Sonny began the meeting, "but I was hoping to get more playing time."

"Well, Sonny, we've talked before that you sub in for Lisa, and she doesn't come out too often. Right?"

"Yeah, Coach, I get it. Keep playing hard, and you'll get your two minutes per game."

"Now, Sonny, that's not what I mean. You know how much I appreciate your hard work and dedication. I wish the whole team had your heart, but sometimes you let your hard work get in the way. You try so hard that sometimes it hurts you instead of helping you."

Seeing a questioning look on her face, Coach continued. "Sonny, I don't want you to stop playing hard. You know what you are doing out there, and I believe in you. It's just that sometimes you try so hard that you make mental mistakes. You should just loosen up and play like you know how."

"Okay, Coach. Thanks. I know my role; I guess I just have to keep reminding myself. I'll try to calm down."

During the next six weeks, Sonny's playing time continued to average around three minutes a game. In March the Lockport Lady Eagles were in the play-offs. They packed the bus for a long tournament weekend at North State, about five hours away. Sonny and Lisa picked seats near each other, so they could talk but still have room to stretch out their 6' and 6'2" frames.

The importance of this weekend was obvious, especially since the team was favored to be Division II champions, but that pressure didn't seem to affect them. For Sonny, her junior year could be the one. This was her last chance to share a championship with her best friend, who would end her basketball career on a high note.

"I want to play so bad this weekend," Sonny told Lisa as the trip to North State began. "I want to feel like I really deserve it, like I've done more than work everyone hard at practice."

"We're gonna get it," Lisa told her, "and you're gonna play!"

Eventually the talk subsided, and Lisa, along with most of the rest of the team, dozed off. Sonny could never sleep on the bus, so from her freshman year on, she would put on her headphones and go over the plays in her mind. She would visualize running the plays and swishing the game-winning shot at the buzzer. Sonny went through her game a couple of times.

After convincingly winning the first three play-off games, tonight was the championship. The team was loose and ready to play. Coach Blair didn't say too much to his team in the locker room. The gymnasium was packed. There were over 5,000 screaming fans. "Check it out," one freshman said, "there's the ESPN booth. This rocks!" The veterans were ready, especially Lisa. Everyone but the freshmen had been here the year before and had played in this gym before; they knew what to expect.

During the first half the lead changed hands many times. At halftime, the Lady Eagles were ahead 48–43. Sonny had actually seen a couple minutes in the first half because Lisa picked up her third foul with 2:04 remaining. In just over two minutes, Sonny made one basket and turned the ball over three times.

At halftime, Coach Blair went over some minor adjustments and let the team know he was proud of them and confident the second half would be their half. He didn't want to get his team overanxious, since they were up as it was. He talked a little about keeping their minds free and staying loose. Then they huddled up, screamed a cheer, and hit the court to shoot around.

As the second half began, the Yellow Jackets came out with a vengeance. They brought the score to within one, then stole the ball. Their star, who usually played post, hit a three-pointer right in Lisa's face. That frustrated Lisa, and she tried to recover her defensive error. In doing so, she committed an offensive foul, her fourth.

Coach Blair believed his girls would respond well, so he decided to save the customary time-out for a bit later. The girls came together with a seven-point run. The score was now 71–67, Lady Eagles in the lead. With 1:30 left in this championship game, Coach Blair called his time-out to give his girls one last breather before the final stretch.

It was the Eagles' ball. The five on the floor tried to work the 30-second clock but wasted too much time and had to throw up a lousy shot at 1:01. The Yellow Jackets rebounded the ball, and their point guard brought the ball up the floor in a hurry. She dished the ball to a teammate who then bounce-passed it in to the girl Lisa was guarding. She gave Lisa a fake that sent her flying in the air, and BAM! Within a few seconds the ball dropped through the hoop, and Lisa was hit with her fifth foul. The score was 71–69 with :47 left to play. The team was devastated, and a look of shock overtook the Eagles' faces. Lisa hardly fouled at all through her four-year career, and she never fouled out. Sonny couldn't believe it. She knew how upset her best friend would be, but she knew it was her time to go in and finish the job.

"Just go in and play your best," Sonny mumbled to herself. "You've worked hard for four years for this moment. Now just go do it!" Sonny jumped off the bench and headed for the scorers' table to report in.

"Hold it a sec, Sonny," Coach Blair said as he grabbed her arm. "Just hold on."

Sonny had no idea what was going on. With a look of wonder on her face, she looked to Lisa for her reaction, but all Sonny got was a sad, tearful look of disappointment. "I always sub for Lisa," Sonny thought. "What's going on?"

Coach Blair called his assistant coaches together and strongly suggested subbing someone else instead of Sonny. They had good bench players, but no one had ever played Lisa's position except Sonny. That is just how it had been for the past three years. Coach Blair continued, "This is the championship game. Our players have to be ready for anything in this last minute plus. Sonny gets too caught up in doing everything perfect. We need someone to just go play!" Coach Blair's 30 seconds were about up. "We have to make a decision!" Coach Blair said to his assistants.

"I say we go with Sonny, Coach," one assistant finally blurted out. Coach Blair looked at the other coaches, waiting for an answer. They just shook their heads in agreement.

"Okay, Sonny, get in there and just play your game." She got a high five from Lisa as she went onto the court.

"Here's your chance, buddy, go get 'em," Lisa yelled before she went to take her seat on the bench. The crowd gave Lisa a grand farewell, with cheers and clapping.

The Yellow Jackets' forward made her free throw and brought the score to within one (71–70). The Eagles now had possession. They were up and wanted an easy basket. Sonny was posting up inside, but her teammates were hesitant to pass it to her. Eventually they did pass it to her, but she was double-teamed, so she passed it back out. When a teammate's shot missed the rim, Sonny had no chance for a rebound, and the Yellow Jackets got the ball.

The Yellow Jackets were in a hurry. They worked the ball around the perimeter, then passed the ball inside to the girl Sonny was guarding. She passed it back out to the Yellow Jackets' best three-point shooter. Sure enough, she buried one. The score was now 71–73, the Eagles trailing. The crowd was on its feet. The players on both benches were kneeling in such a way that they all could have been praying. Fourteen seconds were left on the clock.

The Yellow Jackets set up their press, but the Eagles easily broke it. The point guard threw a long pass to Sonny, who was open on the baseline under the hoop. Her girl had left her alone.

"Oh my goodness," Sonny thought. "Everything seems to be in slow motion." The spectators' screams were muffled, and all Sonny could hear was her own voice saying, "You better catch this!" And she did! Sonny caught the ball, took one dribble and laid the ball in off the glass. As she did, she was fouled. The score was tied 73–73, and Sonny had the chance to put them up by one with only :03.3 remaining. The Yellow Jackets' coach called a time-out in hopes of "icing" Sonny. The crowd was on its feet for good now. Sonny's teammates just about knocked her over when she got to the bench.

"Just do your routine and put it in. Don't think about it," Sonny kept telling herself. When she got to the line, Sonny took three dribbles, spun the ball, positioned her hand just so, and let it go.

It spun in the rim and just seemed to continue spinning. Finally it spun out. After the Yellow Jackets rebounded the miss, they called time-out. They set up and ran a play to the player Sonny was guarding. She caught the ball near the free throw line, faked a shot, and got an anxious Sonny to jump up in the air and foul her on the way down, similar to Lisa's last foul. Just then the horn went off. With no time left on the clock, and everyone standing on the sidelines, the Yellow Jackets' forward sank her first of two free throws, and the game was over.

"So after all of this," Sonny told me, "I don't know if I can play basketball my senior year. I mean, I have a great time with my teammates, but now that Lisa will be gone, and knowing how much my poor play let the team down both on offense and defense, I just don't see the point of going through seven disappointing months and having little or nothing to show for it. I'm thinking I should just hang it up. What do you think?"

Sonny now awaits your response. As a sport psychology consultant, what would you say to her?

Question Guide

1. Describe the characters in this case.
   A. Sonny
   B. Lisa
   C. Coach Blair
2. Describe the main issues in this case. How would you prioritize the issues?
3. What are some possible reasons for Sonny's lack of performance on the basketball court?
4. As a sport psychology consultant, generate some courses of action that might assist Sonny.
5. How feasible is each course of action?
6. What are the ramifications for Sonny of each course of action?
7. As a sport psychology consultant, would you involve Coach Blair in your discussions with Sonny? Why or why not?
8. How would you help Sonny decide whether to play next season?
9. Describe any areas of conflict in the coach-player relationship.

10

DISCIPLINE

Rotella's Insights
and Observations

Discipline is, in many ways, about self-denial of immediate wants and needs in exchange for the attainment of long-term desires. It is in some ways about the ability to delay gratification, but it is never denial for the sake of denial. It is denial for a purpose that is part of a plan with specific priorities. Athletes who view others as terribly disciplined often think that they are making a great sacrifice. In reality, they are simply doing what they love doing and are doing so gladly and freely.

To Tell or Not to Tell

Morris Pickens

THE BOY'S GOLF TEAMS from Elmwood High and Seneca High were on their way back from a Friday golf match in Myrtle Beach. Since Elmwood and Seneca were only a few miles apart, the two teams often traveled together for away matches. The members of the two teams decided that after Elmwood's prom Friday night, they would meet at Elmwood around 11:00 P.M. and then go to someone's house to party. The teams arrived back in town and then split up until later.

The guys on the Seneca team decided to get a little start on the party while the Elmwood team went to their prom, so they met at Sam's house for some night golf. Night golf was just a bunch of putting matches on the fifth green adjacent to Sam's house. The putting wasn't all that important; it was just an excuse to get out of the house, drink some beer, and shoot the bull about whatever and whoever. After two hours of putting, talking, and drinking, Sam, Jay, Rick, and Tom decided to go meet the Elmwood team as planned. Since Jay's car was small and he had his books and clubs in the passenger seat, he decided he would go ahead and round up the Elmwood team at the high school. Tom and Rick stayed with Sam to lock up his house, and then the three left to meet everyone at Elmwood.

As Tom, Rick, and Sam were going down Water Street, they noticed some cars stopped up ahead and flashing lights from a police car. Immediately they all thought the same thing: Jay's been stopped for drunk driving. Jay had had a lot of beer playing night golf, and he was notorious for driving fast. As they got a little closer to the scene, though, they realized that it was worse; Jay had flipped his car over and had almost gone into the river next to the road. Knowing that they couldn't be of much help with the police and ambulance already there and that they were also driving after they had been drinking, Sam, Rick, and Tom went on to let the Elmwood team know what had happened.

At school Monday, Jay was called into the principal's office. Dr. Smith wanted to know what had happened Friday night after the teams got back from the golf match. Jay explained that the two teams had planned to get together after

Elmwood's prom and relax at someone's house. Jay told Dr. Smith that while they were waiting for the prom to be over, the Seneca team had decided to play night golf, and there had been drinking. Dr. Smith reminded Jay that drinking was a violation of the Athlete's Code of Conduct and suspended him from the team for the remainder of the season. The principle asked Jay who else on the team had been drinking Friday night, but Jay would not answer. He told Dr. Smith that he was a member of the golf team, not a member of the faculty and that according to the Athlete's Code of Conduct, he did not have to report other athletes' actions as faculty did. Dr. Smith knew that Jay was correct according to the Code of Conduct, so he dismissed him from his office.

Tom, Rick, and Sam knew that Jay would not rat on them, so they did not say anything else and let the matter pass. The coach for the Seneca team, Mr. Mims, also tried to downplay the incident whenever the media inquired about the team. Mr. Mims was a volunteer coach, and although he knew what went on the night of the accident, he did not report anything to Dr. Smith. He felt it was not his responsibility since he was not on the school faculty. And since he was not on the faculty, he was not subject to the faculty guidelines in the Athlete's Code of Conduct.

The remaining three weeks of the regular season were uneventful. During the fourth week after the night golf incident, Seneca played in the state champion-ship golf tournament and qualified for the All-South Invitational, which includes the four best teams from five southeastern states. After the state championship tournament, however, the night golf incident escalated into much more.

Knowing that the golf team would get a lot more media attention after quali-fying for the All-South Invitational, Jay's parents met with Dr. Smith privately and told him that Tom and Rick had also been drinking the night of the acci-dent. They did not want their son to be the only one singled out for his behav-ior. They also told Dr. Smith that Sam did not drink that particular night because he was taking medication for a cold. Jay's parents made it clear to Dr. Smith that they expected action immediately.

The following morning Dr. Smith telephoned Coach Mims to tell him he had received additional information about the night of the accident. He also asked Coach Mims to schedule a meeting with him "within 48 hours." After getting off the phone with Dr. Smith, Coach Mims calls you, a sport psychology con-sultant who works with the golf team at the university in town. You are now on the phone, and Coach has just told you that he needs to meet with you right away and that it might be best if some of his players met with you also.

Question Guide

1. Describe the characters in this case.
   A. Jay
   B. Jay's teammates (Sam, Rick, and Tom)
   C. Coach Mims
   D. Dr. Smith
   E. Jay's parents
2. Describe the main issues in this case.
3. What are some possible reasons for Jay's decision not to tell?
4. As a sport psychology consultant, generate some courses of action that might assist Coach Mims in sorting out this situation.
5. How feasible is each course of action?
6. What are the ramifications for the golf team members of each course of action?
7. As a sport psychology consultant, would you have Coach Mims or Dr. Smith participate in or attend your discussions with the team? Why or why not?
8. How would you help the team members and Coach Mims decide on the best course of action?
9. Describe any areas of conflict between the coach and the athletes; Coach Mims and Dr. Smith; Dr. Smith and Jay's parents.
10. If Dr. Smith decides to punish Rick and Tom, what should the punishment be? Why?
11. What could Dr. Smith or Coach Mims do to avoid this type of situation in the future?

Cut and Dry???

John F. Eliot

"YEEHAAAAAAAAAAA!" Dirt kicked up furiously as the tires spun. The tailgate of the old pickup flipped open, and the rear end fishtailed across the road.

"Come on, Stretch, knock it off," a voice pleaded from the passenger seat. "You're gonna get us . . . HEY! Watch the trees!"

"Wooooo-eee!" A couple of small branches dropped onto the road as the truck barreled past a row of scrawny maples. A crumpled up tin can flipped out the driver's side window and tumbled off the road into a nearby ditch. "Nobody can stop us, Billy, we're goin' to the show! Crack open a couple more. Woo-hooo!"

"Let me OUT, man . . ."

Brrrrrring, brrrrrring. Brrrrrring, brrrrrring.

The bright red letters displayed 3:43. He groaned, fumbling for the phone. "Hello?"

"Coach McBride?"

"Yeah."

"This is Deputy Drummer down at the station. Sorry to wake you at an hour like this, Coach, but one of your boys is . . . was . . . well . . . Could you come downtown?"

"Huh, what's going on? Who is this?"

"Sir, one of your players . . . I think it would be best if you could come to the station and talk to him."

Coach McBride's senses snapped back quickly. "A baseball player!? Yeah, all right. I'll be there as soon as I can," he rapidly replied, concern evident in his voice.

At 45, being woken up in the middle of the night was the last thing he needed. He had enough stress teaching and coaching in a reform school during the day. Although he was getting used to it, he wasn't fond of doing his job at night, too. But this situation was different. A baseball player was involved.

A 15-minute drive to the police station gave Stanley McBride time to consider what he might find. Most of the students in his high school had been in frequent trouble with the law. This was the reason that the Pearson Correctional High School had been built, and the reason Stanley McBride, a retired Marine sergeant, had a job. This certainly wasn't the first time Stanley had been called downtown during the wee hours of the morning to help a student in trouble. But he was stunned that the officer had said it was one of his players. Since he'd started the Pearson Correctional baseball program four years ago, none of the kids he'd convinced to come out for the team had been in any major trouble. In fact, his track record of keeping kids clean through baseball was the biggest reason he had for turning down some very generous teaching offers at private schools in the country. He knew he was making a difference.

As he pulled into the station parking lot, Stanley was practically blinded by the swirling blue lights of a half dozen cruisers. As he walked across the parking lot, Stan could see a tall skinny kid hunched over in the rear seat of one of the police cars. There was no mistaking this boy. His lean but muscular figure, topped with a distinctive set of dreadlocks, would tell anyone that this was Lane Litkins.

"Coach McBride, thanks for coming down here tonight," Officer Drummer said. "Your boy here decided to go for a little joy ride in his dad's pickup truck tonight. He thought it'd be cool to bring along a little beer. But since he's never given us any trouble before, and since he was outside of town where he couldn't have hurt anyone, we thought you might like to take care of this. I'm sure he won't do it again. You know, he's a good kid and one of your best players, right?"

"I can't believe it! The first one I lose . . . ," Stanley thought to himself as he looked into the dark brown eyes of the boy in the squad car. This kid was one of Coach McBride's biggest success stories, despite a broken home, child abuse, and a gang-run neighborhood. For a few minutes, Coach McBride just looked at his pitcher with a fierce gaze. Inside, he wanted to forgive him. Outside, he knew he must stick to his principles and uphold the team rules. His anger continued to swell.

After a moment's pause, Coach McBride grabbed Lane out of the car and virtually tossed him toward the brick wall of the police barracks. "Lane, how could you pull such a stupid stunt!? I preach to the team every single day about learning respect for yourselves and stayin' clean," Coach McBride hollered, the veins bulging out of his neck. "You know how important your life's gonna be. Why the heck would you wanna go screw it up!?" His face was dark red. "This baseball team, which you were the honored captain of, is the pride of the entire city.

It's a way out. It represents a future for most of the folks around here, even the ones who don't have a dime. You think you can do as you please and everyone'll still kiss your buns just 'cause you got talent? Well, it doesn't work that way. You better start learning 'cause you don't have baseball to hold your little hand anymore. Get your ungrateful crap out of the locker room before tomorrow." Coach McBride stormed across the parking lot and slammed the car door behind him.

Saturday morning came very quickly. Coach McBride had barely an hour's sleep before his alarm clock rang at 6:30. Nevertheless, he was up abruptly, full of energy, as he was every morning before a game. With six years of Marine Corps duty under his belt, Stanley's philosophy on morning behavior was less than surprising. His wife often accused him of being too regimented. He never paid attention. He liked his philosophies; they worked for him.

Stanley combed his hair neatly, with a perfectly straight part on the left side of his head, as always. He was heading for the coffee pot when the phone rang. "Hello, Coach? This here is Mr. Litkins." Coach McBride didn't have a moment's pause to reply. Mr. Litkins continued, "My boy Laney says you kicked him off the team last night. You know he ain't done nothing wrong. He ain't done nothing that his old man wouldn't give him permission to do."

Despite an attempt to cut in, Mr. Litkins controlled the conversation. A well-weathered man in his late 30s, Mr. Litkins had been in and out of jail several times. With no steady income and a nagging addiction to the bottle, his wife had left him in the care of his son long ago. Now that someone was threatening the future of that son, he was going to speak. "You ain't going to shoot my boy's career right in the foot. His old man never got to go to no college or play no professional ball, but he's going to. He's got a future, and you have no right to stand in the way. I expect to see him playing at noon."

The phone clicked. A dial tone resumed before Coach McBride could respond. One down, he thought to himself. Lord knows how many more calls before game time. Having just cut the team's greatest player, he was bound to receive a few phone calls. The telephone rang again.

"Mr. Stanley McBride, please," said an unfamiliar voice. This one was much more pleasant.

"Yes, speaking. What can I do for you?"

"Mr. McBride, this is Dr. Alan Jala. I'm with the Henry James State College Alumni Association. As I'm sure you're aware, one of your players, a pitcher, Lane Litkins, is very well respected by our baseball program here at HJ State. We think he's going to have a big impact on our school's success."

"Yes, I'm aware of your interest in Laney."

"May I speak frankly, Mr. McBride? Well, we have a rather, shall I say, confidential endowment fund here at the Alumni Association. We like to donate money to high schools around the country in need of educational support. Our donations are very well received, and many young athletes who benefit like to return the favor by coming to HJ to get college degrees."

"Are you telling me you want to bribe me so Laney will come play at your college? Is that what this is about?"

"No, no, sir. You see we have already donated a large sum to your high school. We simply heard that some of your players might be in trouble, and we wouldn't want to have to withdraw our donation."

"I've heard enough," Stanley slammed down the receiver. It all seemed to make sense to him now. The Pearson Correctional High School had been making a large number of renovations in the past school year. The facilities were improving rapidly, and the baseball budget had nearly quadrupled. No wonder, thought Stanley. If there was one thing he despised, it was a free lunch. He was trying to teach troubled young men how to work hard for themselves. He surely didn't want someone to waltz in and set back his hard-fought progress of four years.

Before Stanley could finish that thought, the phone rang again. "Coach, it's Reggie."

"Hi, Reg. What are you doing up so early? The game isn't until noon, and we don't have to be on the field until ten. You should still be resting."

"Coach, I'm sorry. But I heard about Stretch, Coach. He's, umm, our best player. And, and, Coach, we had a shot at winning the state title this year. We'll start losing, Coach. If, if we don't make it to the play-offs, a whole lot of guys say they're gonna quit, Coach."

"Reg, calm down. I'll talk to the team first thing when we get into the locker room, okay?"

"But, Coach, if the team falls apart, I'll, I'll never make it to college."

"Reg, I'm really busy this morning. We can talk about it later. Just get ready to play your best. Good-bye, Reggie." Coach McBride had to cut the phone conversation short. Reginold Eiresby was a notoriously nervous young man. When he was only eight, Reggie watched his father die of a heart attack. He thought it was his fault, and as a result, he had grown up trying to be perfect 100 percent of the time. He wanted to make up for it and make his dad proud. Reginold wanted very desperately to go to college, and unfortunately, he was right. He would need an exceptionally good baseball season for recruiters to even notice him. He would certainly not be able to go to college on anything less than a full scholarship, a rare commodity for a student from a school like Pearson High.

Just as Stanley hung up the phone, it rang again. His wife picked it up this time. "It's for you," she called out to Stan.

"Take a message, dear? Thanks."

It was 8:30 A.M. He splashed a little cool water on his face and folded the day's newspaper up under his arm. Stanley walked back into the kitchen where his wife, Sheila, was cooking breakfast. He paused to recall his wish that he could finally build her that dream house in the country because Sheila was so scared of the city. It bothered him that since he had turned down the last offer to move to a private school more than a year ago, no other offers had come in. He wondered if he would be unable to get work now if something were to happen to his current job.

"Who called, dear?" Stanley asked.

"Just then? It was Berry something, I think, from the town council. He sure had a lot of nerve. He wouldn't wait for you, and he started telling me how important baseball was to him and to this town, and how important the upcoming state tournament is. He went on quite a bit about how the citizens of this city deserve the best, or something. I didn't like his tone at all, and I stopped listening to him."

"I'm sorry you had to take that, hon. Some people just have no consideration. I'll get the phone from now on."

Once again, the phone rattled. For goodness' sake, Stan thought, you try and live by an honest philosophy of life, and everyone wants to be your critic. Who else could possibly want to bite my head off? The phone's ringing filled the kitchen. He grabbed the receiver. On the other end, Pearson Correctional High School's senior headmaster spoke in a gruff, serious voice. "McBride? Stanton, here. I need to see you in my office at ten o'clock sharp." The phone went dead.

Stanley pushed the receiver button, got another dial tone, and now your phone is ringing.

Question Guide

1. Describe the characters in this case.
   A. Lane
   B. Lane teammates (Billy, Reg, etc.)
   C. Coach McBride
   D. Lane's father, Mr. Litkins
   E. Alan Jala
   F. Senior Headmaster Stanton
2. Describe the main issues in this case.
3. How does Coach McBride's role relate to team discipline?
4. As a sport psychology consultant, generate some courses of action that might assist Coach McBride.
5. How feasible is each course of action?
6. What are the ramifications for Coach McBride, the team members, and the school of each course of action?
7. As a sport psychology consultant, would you involve Lane or the team members in the discussions between McBride and the headmaster? Why or why not?
8. How would you help Coach McBride decide on the best course of action?
9. Describe any areas of conflict between the coach and the athletes; the coach and the headmaster; the coach and Lane's father; the coach and Alan Jala; and the coach and the townspeople.
10. What can Coach McBride do to avoid this type of situation in the future?

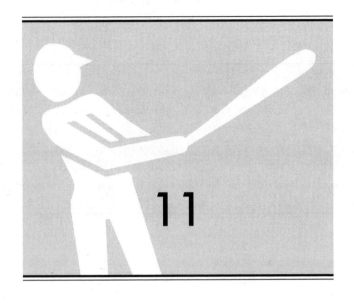

ETHICS

Rotella's Insights
and Observations

Winning is meaningful only if it is done within one's value system and ethical standards. Playing within the agreed-upon rules of the game and giving fellow competitors the same respect expected from them are central to being an ethical competitor. Wanting to win honestly must always be valued more than winning if one is to be considered an honorable and healthy competitive person and role model.

Practice What You Preach

Morris Pickens

I KNOCKED ON THE HOTEL door, expecting a voice from inside the room to invite me in. Instead, I heard the door being unbolted and unlatched and a lot of movement from inside the room. As the door was opened, a voice yelled out, "It's only Tom, our mental coach. You can bring the stuff back out." As I entered the room, I saw Hal, the coach of the golf teams, and players from the men's team pull beer out from under the bed and uncover cards and money on the small table in the middle of the room. They asked me to join in, but I declined, saying that I had had a long trip and thought I would just get a bite to eat and turn in.

After I checked into my room, I ordered room service and watched a little television. As I thought about the scene I had just witnessed, my initial reaction was, "Good grief! I can't believe the coach acts that way around his players." I was about to fall asleep when there was a knock at the door. I thought it must be Hal, who was supposed to be my roommate. I hoped we could talk for a while about our first season working together and the progress the teams had made. Since I had only been working with the teams for seven months, I was still learning what was helpful with which players.

When I opened the door, however, it wasn't Hal, but his fiancée, Candy. She came in and put her suitcase in the corner of the room. She said she had just seen Hal in one of the players' rooms and that he would be joining us in a little while. Hal joined us in about 15 minutes and said he hoped I didn't mind if his fiancée stayed with us, since they hadn't seen each other in a while. I assured him I didn't and that I looked forward to spending time with them the next few days.

I awoke the next morning about 8:30. Hal and Candy were not awake yet and I didn't know what time the teams were scheduled to play their practice rounds, so I caught up on some of my graduate work and let Hal and Candy sleep. At 10:00 A.M. there was a loud knock at the door. When I opened it,

Brenda, a member of the women's golf team, asked why we weren't at the van yet; we were supposed to leave at 10 o'clock for the women's 11:00 A.M. match against North Carolina Tech. Hal woke up, looked at the clock, and exclaimed, "Oh, my gosh! Why didn't someone come wake us up earlier?" As he fumbled around trying to find some clothes to wear, he told Brenda to take the women's team for breakfast in one of the vans and then come back to pick us up.

When the women's team came back from breakfast, Candy got in the van with them and left for the course. Hal, I, and the men's team loaded the other van to head for the course. After a quick breakfast at McDonald's, we raced the 32 miles to the course, making it in about 20 minutes. Hal apologized for such a crazy start to our weekend, but "what could we expect, staying at a small hotel with no wake-up-call service?" On the way over, Hal explained that he wanted me to play a practice round with the men's team, and once he started the women off for their match, he would join us.

When we arrived at the course, I watched both teams hit balls and talked with a few players about the upcoming tournament. Hal explained that he had had a misunderstanding with the coach of North Carolina Tech, so the women's match would not start until noon. Therefore, the men's team went ahead and started their practice round at 11 o'clock. I intended to wait on Hal and join the men's team after the women's match started because I wanted to talk with two of the players about the upcoming tournament. They had both recently suffered injuries and were questioning their "feel" with their short game. However, Hal said he would rather have me play the entire practice round with the men's team, so I went ahead with the men.

On the fifth hole, Hal joined us and said that the women had just started their match. I asked where Candy was, and he explained that since he was with the men's team, he sent Candy to follow the women's match. When we finished, I went with a few of the male players to work with them on their putting while we waited for the women's team to finish. Hal took a cart to follow the women for the last three holes.

That evening, Hal decided to have separate meetings for the two teams. After the women's meeting, I remained to talk with Jill, the women's number one player, about the wrist injury she was recovering from. While we were talking, the phone rang. I answered it and immediately recognized Hal's voice on the other end. "Come on down to room 201 so we can get the men's meeting started. Tell Jill you'll talk with her more later." I said okay and explained the situation to Jill. Judging by her facial expression, this was not the first time her concerns had to wait for those of the men's team. As I walked down the hall to the men's meeting, I thought, "Geez, I sure wouldn't want to be a female golfer here!"

The main topic of the men's meeting was that all season long players had made stupid mistakes and that this weekend we had to have smart play to score well. Hal talked at length about making smart decisions on the course and staying away from any distractions that might cause the players to play poorly. He reminded them that the goal of the team was to play great and that to do that, they needed to focus on their golf game and not let anything interfere with their preparation. The meeting concluded, and Hal and I returned to our room.

Since it was already 10:30 P.M., I thought Hal and I would talk a little more about the upcoming tournament. Instead, Hal suggested I join Candy and him for a drink in the lounge. I declined, saying that I wanted to go back and talk some more with Jill and then I needed to make a few phone calls. He seemed disappointed that I declined but said, "Okay. Remember, we leave at 6:00 A.M. for our 8:00 A.M. tee time." I wondered to myself how much Hal had listened to his own speech about being smart and staying away from distractions.

For the first day of the tournament, I followed the men's team mostly. I saw two female players on two separate holes but did not see the other three women at all. Since the players on the men's team had called and written me much more often than the female players (only one of whom had called me during the season), I thought it was appropriate to spend more time with the men.

Both teams played well the first day, and the men were in second place after shooting their best score of the season. That night, Hal decided to have a joint meeting with both teams after our cookout dinner. Again the meeting was about playing smart. Hal stressed that we needed to stay focused because we had only played well for one day and anything could still happen. During the meeting, Hal finished a beer he had started during dinner. I wondered to myself how serious the players could be when their coach was, in my opinion, setting a poor example.

After the meeting, I talked with a few players from both teams about staying relaxed for the rest of the tournament. Hal and Candy went for a walk along the lake next to our cabins. When they returned, Hal asked how the talks had gone and remarked that he hoped the kids could stay focused for the remainder of the tournament. Since I was leaving the next day and would not be around for the final day, he asked if I had any advice for him about preparing the team for the final round. Specifically, he wanted to know how I felt he should act to bring out the best in his players. How would you respond in my situation?

Question Guide

1. Describe the characters in this case.

   A. Coach Hal

   B. The sport psychology consultant, who narrates the story

   C. Candy, Hal's fiancée

   D. Members of men's and women's teams

2. Describe the main issues in this case.

3. Did the coach's behavior affect his athletes? Should the coach have behaved differently? If so, how?

4. As a sport psychology consultant, generate some suggestions for the coach.

5. How feasible is each suggestion?

6. What are the ramifications of each suggestion?

7. How should the sport psychology consultant have treated Jill? Should he have spent equal amounts of time with the women's and men's teams? Why or why not?

8. Does the fact that the sport psychology consultant is a graduate student affect what he should say to Hal?

Too Good to Be True

Jacqueline C. Savis

"HELLO. BRAD COURTLAND here," I mumbled into the receiver as I reached for the bedside lamp.

"Yeah, this is Vince Mastriani. My hitting coach says you can help me. I know it's late, but I really need to get things turned around. I want things like they always were, you know, when things came easy, when I was the toughest in the majors. I don't know, things just gotta change. You think we can set up a time to meet?"

I might have been half awake a minute ago, but I was wide awake now. Vince Mastriani, "the Maestro" to the baseball world, was calling me up. Sure, everyone knows his name, but no one has followed the Maestro's career like I have. As a sport psychology consultant, I have always revered athletes. With the Maestro, I have always been a fan.

After a deep breath, I found the words. "No, no. Don't worry about it being late. So, Jerry suggested you get in touch with me? He's a great guy and a heckuva coach. Did he tell you a little bit about my work with athletes?"

"Yeah, I mean, he said you worked with some other pro teams, but mostly individual players, and that you're not into all that 'psycho-babble' stuff. He says you can help me get my confidence back, get my swing back."

"Well, we certainly can work on that. Listen, Vince, I'm attending a conference in California in two weeks. Do you want to set something up for then or get together sooner?"

"We've got an off day after we play two games with New York. I'm really anxious to get going on this, before, you know . . . Okay, here's my home number where you can reach me when you arrive in San Diego."

I said that would be fine, and Vince gave me his address in California, some 2,400 miles away and three time zones behind me. I stared at the phone a good 20 seconds after I bid Vince a good-night. How I wanted to wake my wife, Trisha, up! Personally and professionally, this had possibly been the most important five minutes of my life. Could I wait until morning to share my good news? I stared at her, still sleeping, glanced at the clock, which displayed 12:25 A.M., and switched off the lamp. In six hours, she'd be getting our son, Ricky, up. I'd tell her then.

For two hours, I laid awake in bed recalling all the recent articles I had read on the Maestro. Spring training went poorly for him, he was in the last year of his contract, there were clubhouse whispers that his bat speed was shot, etc. Three weeks into the season, he was batting .220, 75 points below his career average, with a mere three RBIs.

There was talk that his many endorsements would start to suffer, but that was just talk. No one, I mean no one, could question the Maestro's appeal, his character. He was a Madison Avenue dream. His lefty swing was almost as picture perfect as the man himself, with his megawatt smile, his Italian good looks, and his 6'3", 200-pound physique. Vince, Rita, and their three kids were featured in many televised endorsements for responsible drinking. The Maestro was also seen in public service announcements for two national youth organizations, extolling the virtues of being honest with yourself and others, being drug-free, and always putting family first.

I glanced at the clock. It was not quite 2:28 A.M., and my thoughts abruptly shifted to myself. At 37, I found my career as a sport psychology consultant really taking off. I was working with professional athletes in four different sports, but primarily with hockey and basketball teams. Baseball, though, had always been my passion, as a player, coach, and consultant. I was in love with my wife of ten years, and I found joy and wide-eyed enthusiasm daily in my eight-year-old's eyes. If that weren't enough, my son and I shared the same enthusiasm for the Maestro. Boy, I thought, I'm going to be "way cool" to Ricky when he finds out who his dad talked to last night!

When 6:30 arrived, I had slept maybe an hour. Trisha kissed my cheek and nudged me to get up. "Honey, did the phone ring last night?" she asked.

Although I should have felt exhausted, I literally hopped out of bed. "Yeah, it sure did, Babe. You'll never guess who it was."

For the next week and a half, I immersed myself in the task of being Brad the observer, instead of Brad the fan. I watched or taped all of the Maestro's games, and I talked to Jerry, his coach, every other day. We set up the day and time that we would all meet in San Diego.

Jerry sounded optimistic that Vince would be receptive. He added that the only thing wrong with his swing was his self-doubt, his lack of confidence. "Yeah, three o'clock on Thursday sounds good, Brad. You know, if things work out, maybe you can work the *rest* of the 'kinks' out of Vince," Jerry said, half chuckling. I hung up the phone, wondering what he meant by this.

The morning arrived for yet another out-of-town flight. Although Trisha had learned to tolerate my frequent business trips, she didn't much care for them. I often considered them a necessary evil, as I had given up the "security" of a university teaching job three years ago to work full-time as a consultant.

"You know, Brad, if things go well with Vince Mastriani, maybe you can introduce him to Ricky when the Padres come here to play," Trisha said while tucking the plane ticket into my jacket.

I took one last swig of coffee, grabbed my keys, and kissed Trisha. "Honey, that's a deal. I'll call you when I land in California. You know, it's only going to be five days."

"Five days is a long time to an eight-year-old, Brad."

"I know, I know. You're right. I'm going to say good-bye to him again."

I bounded up the stairs, two at a time, and walked into Ricky's room. Ricky was crouched on the floor near his bed, looking for something. "Hey, buddy. What are you up to?" I asked.

His small hand reached under his bed and grabbed the Maestro's rookie baseball card, the one I had given him. "Can you get his autograph for me, Daddy? Then next week, I could bring it in to show-and-tell."

Although autograph signing was definitely not on my itinerary with Vince, I couldn't turn my son down. Just one look into those big, brown eyes told me how excited he was and maybe even how proud he was of his dad.

"You be good in school all week, and I'll see what I can do. Okay?"

It was good to see old colleagues and friends of mine at the conference. Privately, I told a couple of my closest friends that I was going to meet with the Maestro on Thursday.

"That guy's loaded. What are you going to charge him?" Ken blurted out.

"Forget about charging him. Just get him to plug you when he gives a television interview. I mean, he's on the tube more than he's on the turf. What does he make? About four million for ball and five for endorsements?" Roz asked me.

"Gosh, I haven't even thought about that. I mean, this is kind of an unusual situation. When I'm working with the teams, I'm always under a contract, seeing them at regular intervals and specific times. This may or may not turn out to be a regular working situation. And, you know, we're talking about the Maestro, here," I offered.

My friends were silent, their eyes squinted, and their heads not quite nodding in agreement with what I had just said. Their silence made me question if I was about to make a big mistake with the Maestro.

It was a short drive from the conference to San Diego. I got ahold of Jerry, and he said to come down to the stadium. Vince would be there, and we could all sit down to talk. Then Vince would maybe take some swings in the cage. Jerry knew that I always preferred being able to see the athlete in his "environment" before agreeing on some program that we'd follow to meet the athlete's objectives.

Jerry greeted me at his office door. It had been nearly two years since I last saw him. He looked more than two years older. He had gone almost completely gray. His slight build was accompanied by the beginning of a potbelly and slightly bowed legs.

I knew Vince's skid had really bothered the coach. "Glad you're here, Brad," he said. "You know, he's still under .230, not to mention the other things."

"What are these other things you're talking about, Jerry?"

"Let's just say that Vince is, deep down, a good guy; he's just not the same guy that everyone thinks he is," Jerry whispered, not making any eye contact with me.

And then, five seconds later, my baseball card took human form and walked toward me. He looked strong, with his jersey clinging tightly to his biceps and chest muscles. But he was in no way larger than life. Those dark, chiseled Italian good looks were there, but where was the disarming smile? Why, I wondered, did his hair appear as if he had just run his fingers through it after waking up? And what was up with the bloodshot eyes?

"Vince, this is Brad Courtland. He's the man you spoke to a couple of weeks ago."

"Right, yeah. Thanks for coming out here and all, but I don't have a lot of time. You think you can just give me your routine, and I can get out of here? I mean, I got a pounding headache, I'm tired as hell, and I gotta meet some other people."

It was immediately apparent what had caused this man's headache, his disheveled look, the bloodshot eyes. My nose could tell me that, and by my guess it wasn't from just one glass of wine with dinner. "Well, we can keep it short today, but I thought you were going to take some swings after we talked."

"For Pete's sake, Vince, the guy's come a long way," Jerry said.

"Fine, sure, let's just get started," Vince grumbled.

I talked to Vince for about 25 minutes in Jerry's office. Once I got over the shock of this "other person," I came to some understanding about what he felt had happened to his swing. He'd become too careful, the pitch had to be too perfect, he got behind in the count, and then he tried to guess pitches. Why he had become too careful, he wasn't sure.

Vince, Jerry, and I left the office and headed to the batting cage. Jerry fed the machine, and Vince hit for about ten minutes. Whaaaack! And the baseball was driven into the netting. "Yep, it used to feel like that!" Vince said during three of his many swings. For 15 minutes we worked on a number of things, including physical and mental routines before his swing.

The three of us walked back up to Jerry's office, Vince and I talking as we went. I asked if he wanted to meet later that day to talk some more, as I was flying back tomorrow. Of course, I also was anxious to define the terms of our working relationship. Was I working for Jerry, for Vince, or for the head coach?

Just as Vince was about to answer, a gorgeous redhead who couldn't have been more than 21 came sashaying around the corner. "There you are, Vinnie. Are you trying to hide from me?"

"Doll, wait in the car. I'll be down in a minute."

This "doll" was definitely not Rita, the adoring wife seen with Vince at all the charity events, seen waiting on him patiently as Vince sips his one glass of wine with his linguine in that television commercial.

"Listen, Brad, I think your stuff can help me. I want to meet with you again. I've been asked to do a charity event near where you live, three weeks from now. It's for an elementary school—something about that if they don't raise money, they'll have to close the school for a month or something. The principal thinks I can draw a good crowd, you know. Nice guy, too. He usually has a bottle of the good stuff waiting for me when I get into town. So, I'm thinking you come with me, you can talk about keeping your head on straight, being committed to what you do, all that jazz, you know, and I give you a cut of what they're going to pay me. You know, kind of like paying you for how you help me. Hell, Brad, if you help me get my swing back, I'll come speak at *your* kid's school. You got kids, right?"

"Well, yeah, but how the heck did you know that?" I asked.

"I mean, I saw you tuck that baseball card away before we went to the cage. Is it your card, or is it your kid's card?" That disarming smile had reappeared on the Maestro's face. "Come on, Brad, you want me to sign it right now?"

The next move was mine.

Question Guide

1. Describe the characters in this case.
   A. Brad Courtland, sport psychology consultant
   B. Vince Mastriani
   C. Jerry, his batting coach
   D. Brad's family
   E. Brad's friends
2. Describe the main issues in this case.
3. How does Brad's admiration of the Maestro affect his working relationship with the athlete?
4. As a sport psychology consultant, generate some courses of action that might help Vince.
5. How feasible is each course of action?
6. What are the ramifications of each suggestion?
7. Should the moral character of the athlete with whom you work affect your working relationship?
8. Would you agree to work with Vince? Why or why not? What would the consequences be if you decided not to work with him?
9. What other information would you need if you were to continue working with Vince?

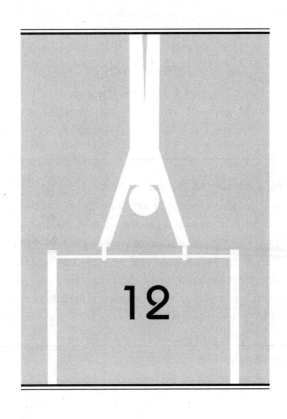

GOAL SETTING
AND PLANNING

Rotella's Insights
and Observations

If an athlete asks whether it is realistic to think that he or she can be an All-Conference, All-American, or All-Pro given a modest past performance, I typically respond by saying, "I have no idea, and I don't care. I want to help you find out if you can be great. I say that to help you believe you can be great and find out if you can be. Let's get into possibilities, not probabilities. Probabilities are for those who wish to play safe and ensure themselves of mediocrity. Let's go for it, and find out how great you can be. Be sure not to create artificial limits."

Squeeze Those Gluts!!!

Stiliani Chroni

"Diana, stop!!!" Coach Francis yells. "What's going on? Why is your routine not coming together? I want you to take a minute, think, and then go for it."

A minute or two later, walking back toward the beam, the coach tells Diana, "Get off the beam, and come here. I know you can do it; you've done all these tricks before. What's wrong now?"

"My body just won't go, Coach," Diana replies. "I'm not letting myself go. I try to think about the trick, and when I believe I'm ready, I just can't go."

"Are you afraid?"

"No, no, I'm not afraid, but I want to make it perfect."

As a child, Diana was one of those kids who loved to run and jump all over the house. She played softball and took jazz dance and ballet classes, but she still had too much energy when she came home. When Diana was 12 years old, her mother decided to get her involved in gymnastics. She hoped that her daughter would tumble on a trampoline instead of her bed and the sofas, and balance on the balance beam instead of their wooden fence. Diana loved it from the very first day. She quit everything else and devoted herself to gymnastics.

Her first gymnastics coach was a wonderful Romanian man who had worked with Nadia Comaneci before Bela Karolyi took over. Working with Coach Pavel meant a lot to Diana, and she learned a lot from him.

At the age of 16, she joined a new gymnastics club team. Her new coach had a negative attitude, and there was no team spirit. Coach Olin was rough with the athletes and believed in "no pain, no gain." No routine ever seemed good enough to him. Diana did not like the new environment, but she loved gymnastics enough to stay with the team until she moved away for college.

She was recruited by Sithonia College (SC), a Division III school. SC has a great reputation for preparing future professionals in the health and physical education area. Attending SC, Diana would have the chance to start for the gymnastics team and also work through a very strong physical education academic program. Diana started competing in the all-around event during her freshman year. She competed in all of the Division III national championships during her freshman, sophomore, and junior years. As a junior, she was awarded All-American Honors. This year, Diana is a senior and the captain of the women's gymnastic team.

Diana has had a chronic problem with her wrists due to weak joints, and the pain has been gradually increasing. She has been performing with supporting braces on both wrists since her freshman year, but on the bars and vault the pressure and the pain became unbearable. During her junior year, Diana and her head coach decided that she should stop competing on bars and vault. Diana was not happy with this decision, but she had no other choice.

Even with her nagging injury, Diana almost always wore a smile on her face. Coach Francis often said she had never known a gymnast with a bigger smile. Especially on floor, Diana's specialty, she would move around as if her whole body were smiling. Diana just dazzled the judges with her floor exercise. At 5'4" and very fit, Diana tumbled and turned on her megawatt smile, while a huge white and maroon hair ribbon mimicked her every step. One of her teammates even kidded Diana that the ribbons and her ear-to-ear grin were worth at least .025 points from the judges!

When Diana started at SC, she enjoyed working with Coach Francis, but recently Diana has sensed that things are changing. Diana feels as if the coach has no time for her. Diana's diary entries this year illustrate her growing concern. "Monday, more 'dirty looks' from Coach. Coach Francis is good. She is a little autocratic, but she knows what she is doing. She may have favorites in the gym, but I know that deep down she cares for all of us. It's just that she does a poor job of expressing it," she wrote.

Now that Diana is a senior, she wants to make her last year as a college gymnast a great one. She has her heart set on being a great team captain and qualifying for Nationals. She also hopes to compete in the all-around again. She would love to finish her career as a *great* all-around gymnast, the best on the team.

Since the start of her senior year, Diana has been experiencing some difficulties with her performance. Suddenly, she misses tricks and moves that she used to perform easily. Her physical condition is not the problem: She is as fit as she has ever been. Her thinking is what is causing her difficulty. Two thoughts cross her mind before executing the tricks: "It has to be perfect," and to a lesser extent, "What if my wrists don't make it through the pressure?"

She is keeping a diary, for practices as well as meets. Every day she writes down what she did in practice, how it was, and how she felt. This log helps her keep track of everything that goes on in the gym. She notes things she could not execute and tricks that she did well. Late in September, she wrote, "These two aerials on the beam have to come together soon; I don't have much time left. I have to connect them smoothly, but I can't do it. I work hard, I stay after practice, but they are not coming together."

This log has been with her at all practices and meets and is one of her rituals. Lately, she has had a hard time keeping up with it. She wants to keep this part of her routine, like the one Tootsie Roll that she treats herself to before performing in a meet.

After some incidents where Diana could not execute her routine, Coach Francis called a meeting with Assistant Coach Reap. "Do you have any thoughts or suggestions about Diana?" Coach Francis asked. "You've worked with her the last three years. She trusts you. Do you see a way to help her with her performance?"

"I think the problem is how Diana sees gymnastics," Coach Reap replied. "Gymnastics is the center of her life. If everything goes okay with gymnastics, then she's fine. If something goes wrong, however, everything goes wrong!"

Apparently, this rule even governs Diana's relationships. Her boyfriend, Marc, told Coach Reap that her obsession for a perfect gymnastic performance has strained their relationship terribly. "If I weren't a perfectionist in athletics myself, I don't think we'd still be dating. I try to respect her commitment, but sometimes she is beyond any limitations. She has her goals set, and nothing can get her mind off of them. Lately, she is more than obsessed with her goals. I try to stay next to her and give her all the support I can. I think this is what she needs from me now."

Coach Francis decided to call Diana in for a meeting. She wanted to ask her what she sees as the problem. Diana told her that she doesn't really know what is going wrong. She talked about the two thoughts that often cross her mind and that she "just can't let go." When talking to Coach Francis, she mentioned her difficulty with visualization, describing it this way: "I used to close my eyes and see myself doing it, executing the routine and each of the tricks. I could feel my body moving, flying. Now I can't!"

Coach Francis suggested to Diana that she forget her goals for a minute. "Get out there and just perform, and bring that smile back, Diana!" After her two meetings, Coach Francis now believes that Diana has become overanalytical in the gym, with herself and with her teammates. She needs to relax and let go. "You have the potential for something great, but only if you stop thinking," Coach Francis said to Diana at the end of their meeting. Somehow, Diana didn't appear convinced.

Recently, Diana has started having negative thoughts about herself. Her confidence is shaky sometimes, like it was when Coach posted the prefinal lineup for this year's first meet. Her name was not on the list, and she was very upset. She believed that she was more ready than some of the women who were in the lineup and that Coach Francis was not being fair. "After all, the coach has not seen all my routines lately," Diana pleaded to Coach Reap.

Diana believes that her motivation has greatly suffered, but she does not want to let anybody down, especially herself. She can understand that not everybody has the same level of commitment, but being the captain she has to try her best. When Diana sees the women of the team forming cliques and cheering only for their buddies, she gets upset. Not everybody perceives the team spirit concept in the same way! Her attitude, her work ethic, and her performance have to be "the best."

Two months after Diana started her senior year, Coach Francis called and asked me, a sport psychology consultant, to meet with Diana. After her meeting with the gymnast, Coach Francis thought that she could use some help with her thinking process. The next day in the gym, she asked Diana if she would like to meet with me to talk about her recent difficulties. Diana said yes, she was willing to try anything that could help her performance.

"Diana is the captain of our team," Coach Francis told me. "We need her, but I'm not sure how far I can trust her. She has had these mental blocks since last spring. Then, however, the blocks were not so bad, and I could work through them. I try to help her now, but nothing seems to work. I let her work alone, and she complains to Coach Reap that I don't care. She's absolutely obsessed with trying to reach her goals! At some point I think she's scared of the freshmen on the team. Being the captain has placed a lot of pressure on her, I'm sure. I really don't know how to handle her anymore. Could you help her through? I can give you her number," Coach Francis said to me, with not-so-subtle desperation in her voice.

Question Guide

1. Describe the characters in this case.
   A. Diana
   B. Coach Francis
   C. Coach Reap
2. Describe the main issues in this case, and prioritize them.
3. What factors contribute to Diana's poor performance in gymnastics?
4. As a sport psychology consultant, generate some courses of action that might help Diana.
5. How feasible is each course of action?
6. What are the ramifications of each suggestion?
7. Are Diana's goals too demanding? How would you help her refocus her goals?
8. What affect, if any, does Diana's practice log have on her performance and attitude about gymnastics?
9. What other information would you need if you were to work with Diana?
10. Would you seek the assistance of other sport-related professionals in order to help Diana?
11. Would you include Coach Francis in your conversations with Diana? Why or why not?

Bye-Bye, Birdie

Kathryn C. Wilder

"Hey, batter, batter. Hey, batter, batter, batter—swing!" the Wayland Little League players chanted in the direction of home plate, where Andrea's blond pigtail poked out of her Cub's cap. In 1977, Andrea became the first girl to play in her town's baseball program.

As a youngster, Andrea always excelled in sports. Her friends and family held lofty expectations for her future achievements. Andrea was always looking for an encore. She was never interested in being just one of the crowd; the limelight suited her just fine.

As a kid, Andrea's inclination to dream complemented her natural athletic talent. Her mantra as a youngster was "I'm going to be a pro athlete." Although Andrea rarely set short-term goals for herself, she had the single-minded focus of being the top performer in the world in her chosen sport. In some ways, her self-identity became intricately connected to her achievements in sport.

In college, Andrea loved being part of a team. She played field hockey in college and was patient in her quest for excellence. She garnered respect from her teammates and coach for being completely "absorbed in the doing." Andrea played in the present and was hardly ever interested in the outcome. The carefree, almost frivolous, attitude that was so evident in her childhood remained with her as an adult. Andrea just went out and played her best, with dreams of one day being able to make a living playing a sport. An observer might conclude either that Andrea was very patient in seeking her dreams or that she was not very directed.

During the summer between Andrea's junior and senior years in college, she turned her energy toward the golf course. Andrea met Jack, a golf pro from South Africa who focused on her as both a person and an athlete. Andrea loved to go out and play the game every day, and Jack instilled in her an awesome sense of self-confidence. "Andrea, you have one of the most natural golf swings that I have ever seen in my life. It would be wasted talent if you didn't give this game a shot."

Andrea practiced every day all summer, and she became enthralled by the game. Like any natural athlete, Andrea knew she had a certain knack for golf. She didn't have any specific goals, but she was focused on her game. Jack and the other golf pros she played with that summer recognized Andrea as having been born to play the game. By the end of the summer, Andrea was playing at a 7 handicap, which impressed her parents and the "loyal supporters" at her club.

During Andrea's senior year of field hockey in college, she was captain of the squad and leading scorer, and she earned MVP honors. Andrea enjoyed her senior year, but she was ready to move on to a new sport upon graduation. On the basis of the positive feedback she had received regarding her golf game, she decided that she could find glory on the golf course. Consequently, when Andrea graduated from college, she decided to chase her dream of becoming a pro athlete.

During Andrea's rookie year as an amateur golfer, she loved every minute of practice and tournament play. She had a Senior Tour player working with her, and he gave her tremendous encouragement and feedback concerning her game.

Andrea shocked some of her competitors by doing very well her initial year of tournament play. For instance, she won the Vermont Women's Amateur Tournament in her first state tournament appearance.

For the last five years, Andrea has been a pro on the mini tour. She has played the Futures Tour, the Asian Tour, and the Gold Coast Tour. Last year she played in approximately 25 events. Andrea describes the tournament atmosphere as "fun and intense at the same time. Everyone jokes around, but you can still feel the nervous energy in the air."

On the tour, Andrea values honesty and a hard work ethic in both herself and her competitors. She admires people who are great golfers because she knows how intensely they have worked to hone their talent. Andrea is happiest when she is succeeding and enjoying the task at hand.

Last fall, Andrea made it to the finals of Q (qualifying) school in Daytona Beach, Florida. She played 72 holes of tournament play and missed the cut by only three strokes. During Q school, Andrea felt a "twinge" of pain shoot up her elbow. Andrea was brokenhearted about missing the cut and then had to deal with the escalation of pain in her elbow.

A physical therapist examined Andrea's elbow and found that she had lateral epicondylitis (tennis elbow). He suggested that she discontinue golfing for six weeks to avoid developing chronic tendinitis. Andrea took from December 1 through January 15 off from golf in hopes of a full recovery. However, the pain in her elbow never did completely subside, and she was able to play just five tournaments from mid-January until April.

Andrea played through the pain for months, expressing her frustration to her friends and family that she couldn't play and practice as she had in the past. Andrea was also anxious about surgery because there was always the thought that maybe she should take the conservative approach and wait out the injury. Ultimately, Andrea trusted her doctor, and in mid-October she had surgery to treat her tennis elbow. During surgery the doctor repaired the large partial tendon tear and removed tissue at the elbow.

The day after the surgery, Andrea suffered from physical pain and emotional turmoil. The throbbing, penetrating ache and the realization that she was "out for a while" had registered with her. It was at this point that Andrea called up a local university to inquire if there was someone in the sport psychology department who could talk to her about her injury. A department secretary recommended Dr. Garth Hall, a faculty member whose research interests were goal setting and psychological rehabilitation from sport injury.

During their first meeting, Dr. Hall asked Andrea a series of questions so that he could better understand Andrea and her situation. The following is a transcript of the interview conducted by Dr. Hall.

Did you see a doctor as soon as you felt pain in your elbow?

I saw a doctor in Florida as soon as my elbow began to hurt me. He had me do rehab before giving me a cortisone shot. After he gave me the cortisone shot, my elbow was perfect again until around mid-April.

Were you concerned about not playing golf again?

The whole situation was so scary because my elbow would be perfect for a few months, and then the pain would recur. It was strange. I kind of had this little twitch, and it just kept coming back.

What were your goals in golf before the injury?

To make the LPGA tour and to make some money back from the Gold Coast Tour, which I had to quit. I believe that it takes 100 percent effort, tournament experience, and consistency in competition to make the tour.

What advice would you give yourself when you started tournament play?

First, don't get caught up in mechanics because you are a total natural. I was gifted in that sense. I left a top teaching pro, and maybe I should have stayed with him. I tried to find the right teacher, so I had six different pros in the last seven years. Second, work more on my short game. Third, concentrate more on visual work. Fourth, eliminate my fear of failure. When I first started, I was just having great fun playing. I would rise to the top. Toward the end, I had more fear and not as much fun with the game. And fifth, set some more specific short- and long-term goals. I don't know, though. I was never really into goal setting."

On the topic of goal setting, what are some of your goals for the next couple of weeks?

Not to be as bored as I have been, and to try and relax without feeling guilty. I should be able to sit at home, prop up my arm, and just relax.

Did the surgeon give you any details regarding what to anticipate in the healing process?

I feel like I'm kind of blind of what to expect. I have a ton of questions to ask my doctor. I'm not sure what to expect, but hopefully, I will be chipping and putting three weeks from now. I think my doctor is pretty conservative, and he says in three months I'll be playing. So, maybe I'll be out there in less time. I'm sure I will.

Do you think the surgeon or the physical therapist would be receptive to helping you form some realistic rehab goals?

Oh, yes. He's a great doctor, and I feel like he treats me like I'm his only patient. I think he will probably guide me, but it's the PT in Florida that will help me out. I could never understand why doctors and PTs don't talk with one another.

In the absolute worst-case scenario, if your elbow didn't fully heal, have you done any searching for an alternative career?

What search? I have tried not to think about it. I've been putting it off. I put together my résumé, and I decided that I did not want to teach golf. The pay is low, and you aren't treated very well. So, I'm hoping that I have one last chance to play golf.

Dr. Hall appreciated Andrea's being so honest and giving him such genuine responses. He felt that she was very receptive to having someone help her with goal setting in both the rehabilitation setting and on the golf course once her injury had healed. Dr. Hall wasn't sure if he should explore Andrea's lack of career aspirations outside of golf, if he should refer her to a career counselor, or if he should just ignore the issue and concentrate on getting her healthy enough to play her sport.

Dr. Hall recognized that Andrea's plans for the near future were put on hold until she met with her doctor. She didn't quite know what to expect regarding her healing process. She was assuming that her cast was going to be coming off in three weeks, but she didn't have much more information.

Put yourself in Dr. Hall's shoes. How would you proceed with Andrea?

Question Guide

1. Describe the characters in this case.
   A. Andrea
   B. Jack, the golf pro
   C. Dr. Hall, the sport psychology consultant
2. Describe the main issues in this case, and prioritize them.
3. As a sport psychology consultant, generate some courses of action that might help Andrea.
4. How feasible is each course of action?
5. What are the ramifications of each suggestion?
6. Will Andrea be receptive to both short- and long-term goal setting? How would you help her refocus her goals?
7. Should Dr. Hall explore Andrea's lack of career objectives outside of golf? Why or why not?
8. What other information would you need if you were to continue working with Andrea?

ATTITUDE

Rotella's Insights and Observations

The longer I live, the more I understand the impact of attitude on life. Attitude, to my way of thinking, is far more important than facts. It is more important than the past, than education, than money, than circumstances, than failures, than successes, than what other people think or say or do. It is more important than appearance, giftedness, or skill. Attitude can make or break an athletic career or a team. The remarkable thing is that we have a choice every day regarding the attitude we will embrace. We cannot change our past. We cannot change the fact that people will act in a certain way. We cannot change the inevitable. The only thing we can do is play on the one string we have—and that is our attitude.

Rough Waters

Stiliani Chroni

"THANK GOD THEY'RE head-racing in the fall meets. At least we won't have to deal with Lisa's bad temper and hysterical reactions if she doesn't row well!!! Head-racing doesn't seem so threatening to her. She prefers it when the boats leave the starting line every 15 or 30 seconds, though I don't understand why." Those were the words that Lisa's father uttered to his wife as they arrived at the start of the first rowing meet of the year.

Lisa is a sophomore at the University of Meteora, a Division I institution. Rowing is a club sport, but the competition is rather keen. Lisa loves the sport, and she wants to do well. Making the U.S.A. National Team for the 2000 Olympic Games is her dream and ultimate goal, although rowing has not always been her sport. Lisa was a swimmer for the better part of her life. It wasn't until the spring of her junior year in high school, after the swimming season was over, that Lisa took up rowing. Initially, Lisa felt awkward as she struggled to learn her new sport. Eventually, the novelty of the whole experience and the absence of pressure made her fall in love with rowing.

At 5'11", Lisa is a tall woman with long limbs and a strong build, although she doesn't look extremely muscular. She is a self-professed introvert and a pessimist.

As a child, Lisa preferred swimming over softball and basketball. She was neither one of the strongest swimmers nor one of the weakest on the team, and swimming was fun for her.

When Lisa went away to a boarding high school, she found herself as one of the best swimmers on the team. It was a whole new experience being one of the best, and that was when things started to change for her. She saw herself becoming a team leader and a role model, and there was a lot of attention paid to her. People actually looked up to her, and that felt wonderful! Under this spotlight, though, some of Lisa's negative traits came out along with the positive ones. During her junior year, Lisa quickly gained a reputation as a whiner, complaining about herself and about the workouts. Even so, she never missed a single practice.

Lisa's constant negativity prompted her swimming coach to point out to her that her attitude was hurting her sport, her teammates, and, more than anything else, Lisa herself. The young swimmer was initially very defensive.

"What do you mean, Coach? How can I hurt my sport when I work so hard? I work harder than anybody else, I'm never late, and I never miss practice. I'm not negative; I just can't tolerate irresponsibility and swimming poorly. Can't you see how important practices and meetings are for me?"

Lisa did not want to accept her coach's comments as truth, and before he could finish, she ran out of his office and back to her room. Lisa called her mother, whom she knew would listen and understand her. After a brief conversation that didn't do the trick, Lisa took some time to reflect on her coach's words. Could he possibly be right?

Lisa called her coach the next morning and set up a second meeting. With a concerned and less defensive tone in her voice, Lisa started the meeting off by asking, "What do you mean when you say I'm negative, Coach? What do you think I'm doing to hurt myself, my team, and my sport?"

Coach Larry was more than glad to explain his thoughts to Lisa, since she hadn't given him a chance to do so the day before. It was after this second meeting that Lisa decided she really needed to work on her attitude. She tried to stop complaining, she tried to listen and use her coach's technical instructions and corrections, and she tried to broaden her definition of success.

That year, with a lot of effort, she was able to make an attitude adjustment that lasted for the rest of her high school junior year. The year ended successfully with the New England Swim Championships, where Lisa had her best times for the year. Even though she did not win any of her events, Lisa was genuinely thrilled with her success.

This newfound success and satisfaction were short-lived. Her senior year in high school brought a reversal of fortune for Lisa. Her attitude was negative once again, and her times were getting worse. She was carrying the success of her junior year like a leaden weight on her shoulders. Lisa constantly worried about letting down her team, coach, or parents. She felt Coach Larry was placing more and more pressure on her. "Come on, Lisa. You've got to work hard," he told her. "This year you can win the New England Championships. This is your big chance!"

This was Lisa's last year as a high school swimmer; she had to do well. Each meet seemed to be a matter of life or death. Suddenly, swimming was a big deal, and everything (her life, her moods, her attitude) depended on her meet times.

What was once new and fun was now old and tiring. Her performance, her times, and her meet results meant a lot more than they had ever before. On top of that, it was becoming increasingly difficult for Lisa to control her emotional outbursts. Senior year ended "unsuccessfully" for Lisa. Not only did her times not improve, but they went up.

Lisa decided to stay away from the pool for a while. One of her friends had joined the high school crew team during their junior year and had always told her how much fun rowing was. Lisa needed a change. Rowing sounded like a great idea for a spring sport and as a getaway from the pool.

The following year, Lisa started her college career at the University of Meteora. She believed she was accepted because her father was an alumnus, she was an in-state applicant, and the university needed people for the rowing team. With no confidence in herself and a negative attitude lingering from swimming, she rowed crew for the novice team her freshman year. Since she had some rowing experience, she became the "stroke leader" for the novice team.

Lisa's attitude, however, was no better than it had been her senior year in high school. She complained regularly, but she still did not miss any practices. Frequently, she would get extremely upset with her performance, scream at her teammates as if it were their fault, and cry as if the world had come to an end.

At an erg test (a timed performance test on an ergometric rowing apparatus) that helped the coaching staff assess the team's performance, Lisa was a quarter of the way into the test when suddenly her body seemed to shut down. She finished the erg test but at a considerably slower pace. As soon as she finished, she felt despondent, ran out into the freezing cold crying hysterically, threw herself down on the cold grass, and began rolling back and forth. Both Claire, her roommate, teammate, and close friend, and Coach Stevens ran after her, but they could not console her. All she could think was that she was a failure, a quitter, and that her life was ruined. She refused to listen to them or to go back into the gym. Walking back to her room alone, Lisa crawled into her bed and stayed there for the next two days, convinced she was a loser!

Incidents like this were not infrequent. Lisa was devastated when her boat came in fourth at the spring championships because she had been convinced that the team would win. In response, she screamed at her teammates and cried. She blamed everybody on the boat, including herself.

Lisa is a sophomore this year, and she is rowing for the junior varsity team as the "fifth man," (a strong rower). Coach Stevens approached Lisa in the middle of the fall semester and asked for a meeting. Lisa respects and admires her coach very much, but this request for an individual meeting made her uptight.

Lisa walked into Coach Stevens's office at the boathouse, feeling a little scared and insecure, not knowing what the meeting was about. "Lisa, I think you can become a great rower," Coach Stevens began. Lisa smiled and opened her eyes and ears, waiting for his next comment.

"Your lean, long limbs are perfectly suited for rowing. You work very hard, and you never skip practice. But from my own experience, I know that hard work is not everything. You need to believe in yourself and trust your abilities. Since you have a dream to become a national rower, you have to work for this dream, not only by practicing every day but by remembering your dream every day and believing that you can do it. If you have a bad day in practice, that doesn't make you a loser. . . . When I comment on your technique or performance, you shouldn't get upset and defensive. Instead, you should use the information for your benefit."

Coach Stevens suggested that Lisa may want to talk with one of the sport psychology consultants at Meteora. He believed that Lisa would be able to make some essential changes with a little help. Specifically, the way she treated her teammates, herself, and the sport should be more consistent. One day she loves it, and the next day she wants to quit. "This is not the attitude that a rower with dreams should have," concluded Coach Stevens.

That was it! Coach Stevens started with a positive comment but once again, like in high school, her coach was seeing something wrong in her attitude. "I'm a loser once again," Lisa concluded.

On her way to class after the meeting, she stopped by the weight room, hoping Claire would be there. She wanted to talk to someone, but not just anyone. Claire saw her every day—in classes, in practice, at home—and maybe she could help Lisa understand. Claire was there, and Lisa gave her all the details of her meeting with Coach Stevens.

Claire knew what Lisa wanted to hear, but she also knew how hard practice was with Lisa. Claire thought for a minute and then decided to speak her mind.

"Look, Lisa. Remember last Friday when we were rowing and you were literally screaming at the rest of us, 'You guys don't pull hard enough! This is not right! That's wrong!' and you went on and on? Well, you can't do that. We're trying our best. If you have something to say, at least wait until after practice. We can't concentrate with your voice in our ears. You talk about what we do wrong, and when the coach corrects something on you, you get so upset!

"I know you wanted to talk to me because I'm your friend, but I had to talk about all this, too. I like you, but rowing in the same boat is like a nightmare some days. One coach is enough. This is what coach saw and why he called you for a meeting. He wants to help you and the team. Don't take it the wrong way and start that being-a-loser thing again. Come on, you can do it. We can do it!"

Lisa could not believe her ears. "I don't want to be a nightmare for my boat-mates," she thought. "I can be good. I work hard, but this is not the key to success. I must believe in myself. I am not a loser." What a day! The confusion was a nightmare! Lisa knows that big changes are coming up next year, and she had better be ready. Women's crew will become a varsity sport starting next year. This change will be a critical one because the team will have to work harder and be there 100 percent, physically and mentally.

Lisa walks up the stairs to the Health and Sport Sciences Department, not really knowing what to do. "Maybe the sport psych people can give me an answer," she thinks. If Lisa walked into your office, recounted her case to you, and asked for your help, how would you proceed?

Question Guide

1. Describe the characters in this case.
   A. Lisa
   B. Lisa's parents
   C. Coach Larry
   D. Coach Stevens
   E. Claire
2. Describe the main issues in this case, and prioritize them.
3. As a sport psychology consultant, generate some courses of action that might help Lisa.
4. How feasible is each course of action?
5. What are the ramifications of each suggestion?
6. How would you talk to Lisa about the attitude change she needs to make without her interpreting this conversation in terms of her failure as a rower?
7. Anticipate habits that might hinder Lisa from making the desired changes, and plan for overcoming her self-defeating tendencies.

Riding out of Her Mind

Kathryn C. Wilder

THE COOKIE LADY stood at the mountain's summit, waved her arms, and cheered, "Hi, Chrissy. I brought homemade cookies and lemonade for you and all your friends." Chrissy was leader of 13 exhausted adults who were on day seven of a 90-day bicycle trip across America. She was the youngest leader ever of a trans-America tour, but she had had many prior bicycle-touring experiences all over the world. By the age of 22, Chrissy could say, "My bicycle's odometer reads over 20,000 miles, more than the miles logged on my car's odometer."

Chrissy had always loved sports and had a strong sense of commitment to achieving her goals. As the youngest of six children, Chrissy soon focused on running faster, being stronger, and being more coordinated in order to keep up with her siblings. She loved playing hide-and-seek, climbing the jungle gym, and playing other neighborhood games. Early on, she savored the *sweet taste of success* in sports and other physical games. Speed, thrill, and movement lent to the satisfaction; not surprisingly, she wanted to be the best in her chosen sport.

In her adulthood, Chrissy has kept alive the spirit of her childhood. She has chosen not to be "realistic" but to believe in her dream of being a nationally ranked cyclist. Chrissy has continued to believe that she has the physical strength and mental power to be committed to excellence in cycling. Her devotion to cycling even surpassed a major health-related setback. However, she felt that meeting with a highly recommended sport psychology consultant, Dr. Tucker Landon, would help her with an "attitude adjustment." Dr. Landon has consulted with competitive cyclists in the past, and he interviewed Chrissy to discover what makes her tick.

How do you use your mind to be the best competitor you can be?

Tapping into my mental and physical capacities to excel is not always simple. I must constantly focus on my strengths and take full responsibility for how I think about myself. The bottom line is that I truly believe that I have the freedom to achieve what I want in life."

On a scale of 1 to 10, how do you rate your commitment to fitness?

On a scale of 1 to 10, my lifetime commitment to fitness rates a 9. I am very focused; however, my motivation has become based on intrinsic rather than extrinsic rewards. I enjoy intensity, commit to a task, and desire a high level of self-awareness. I want to go beyond the boundaries of my potential by developing an innate ability to forgive and forget and to learn from past mistakes or setbacks in sport.

In the past, what have been some of your motivational tendencies?

In competitive cycling, I'll only compete if I know that I'm in top physical condition. In the future, I must be careful not to let this self-doubt of actual fitness level allow me to throw away my dreams. I believe that my enthusiasm and sheer love of my sport will provide me with the desire to achieve my ambitions.

Are you mentally and physically committed to achieving your aspirations?

I have the discipline for doing the hard training and mental preparation; however, there is a time commitment involved that I'm not sure I can meet while in graduate school. Ultimately, I'll enjoy the process and challenge of getting to the top.

Why do you enjoy cycling so much?

When in top physical condition in cycling, I can, as the Nike motto says, 'just do it.' Riding through a foreign environment brings me joy, exhilaration, and a sense of reckless abandon.

Does your self-motivation always help you? When has it hindered you?

I can stay motivated to the point of always taking on more than anyone else could possibly handle. In order to reach my dream, I must achieve a level of awareness that enables me to rest my body under stressful situations.

Dr. Landon discovered that in the past, Chrissy's perfectionist tendencies may have caused her to overcommit herself in sport. The following historical perspective is based on information gathered by Dr. Landon throughout the course of their interview.

Chrissy graduated from college in December. She had only been racing competitively for one and a half years when she decided that she would train full-time with elite cyclists. In January, she moved to Florida and trained with top riders. She trained seven days a week, riding an average of 50 miles a day. Intense weight training three times a week was also part of her schedule. Even though the demands were often heavy and challenging, she kept up with some of the best female cyclists in the country.

Past experiences in sport provided positive reinforcement for Chrissy. She felt that she had the capacity to give more of herself in comparison to others. Almost overnight, Chrissy's world became cycling. She was improving rapidly and became obsessed with being one of the top cyclists in the world.

Chrissy met her short-term goals of placing in the top five in races that attracted elite-level cyclists. She climbed from being a CAT 4 cyclist to a CAT 3 and was on the cusp of gaining professional level CAT 2 status when her body became worn down by fatigue after six months of rigorous, daily training sessions. (The CAT [category] 1–4 rankings are based on a point system established by the U.S. Cycling Federation, which governs both amateur and professional cycling in the United States.) Her burning desire to excel had blinded her to the physiological signals from her body. After being dropped early from a race in California, she visited a local hospital for a complete physical analysis.

Chrissy was devastated when she was told that she had mononucleosis. Her outer shell appeared strong and invincible, but internally she was worked thin with fatigue. Chrissy wondered, "Have I failed myself by becoming so focused on achieving my goal? Did I train too hard too soon?" Chrissy wanted to push herself to higher levels, but her body would not respond to her desires.

After six weeks of sleeping 14 to 16 hours a day, Chrissy became fearful that the virus that had sought refuge in her body would revive if she resumed a full-time training schedule. As a result, she turned her energy to her new job in a start-up sports marketing firm, working for her lifelong pro basketball hero. Once again, Chrissy immersed her heart and soul into another task. She worked with the marketing firm for roughly two years before enrolling in graduate school. With work and school demands as they were, a return to competitive cycling would have to wait.

Chrissy went back to graduate school in September and vowed that she would do her best to find the time to train and compete again in cycling. Nevertheless, the transition to graduate school, the desire to earn a high GPA, and a substantial video-production project took precious training hours away from her schedule. It wasn't until the next September that Chrissy reworked her time commitments and followed through on her promise to herself to compete again in cycling.

Chrissy recently finished off a successful season, competing in nearly 60 races over a six-month period. She earned the titles of District Criterium Champion and Atlantic Coast Cycling Conference Champion, received All-American Honors, was voted the top cyclist in two states, and was upgraded to a CAT 2 racer.

Chrissy was very pleased about the results of her first year back in racing, especially since she carried a full course load in graduate school. When she officially finished her racing season, she refocused her energy on endurance training to help build a base for the next year of racing. She was also cross-training for a greater variety in her workouts. She started running and mountain biking in addition to doing long-distance workouts on her bicycle. She participated in a few centuries and shattered the 100-mile course record in only her third century race.

Ring, ring, ring. Chrissy was on her way to class when the phone rang, and she thought twice before finally picking it up.

"Hi, Chrissy. This is Linda Jackson. How would you like to race for Team Lotus at the National Pro Criterium Championship? We'll pick up all of your expenses. You've had a terrific season, and we want you to race for us."

Chrissy was psyched. Who in their right mind could turn down an all-expense paid trip to Colorado with some of the best racers in the world?! If nothing else, it would be a great learning experience for her, and she did love criterium racing.

Still, Chrissy wanted to give herself a chance to think about it. "Linda, it sounds like a really great opportunity. I'm a bit skeptical though, 'cause you see, I've already changed my focus for the season. I haven't done any high-intensity speed work or racing since mid-August," Chrissy explained.

Linda understood Chrissy's concerns, but she still thought that it would help a couple of the Team Lotus racers if Chrissy were there.

"Listen, Chrissy. I think having you at the race will help out Suzi and Nina. Neither of them have been at a major competition before. I think just your being there will help them feel a little more at ease about racing. Anyway, whatever you decide, I need to have an answer within the next 24 hours, so I can contact someone else if you can't make it."

Chrissy had to make a decision—and fast! She knew that she would excel at an aggressive fast-paced criterium, which is a multilap race, usually on downtown streets. The sudden attacks that rapidly accelerate the pace of the field and the individual and team tactics that all influence the race help create a dynamic and exciting event. The bright colors and sponsorship logos on team uniforms make it easy to determine who your competitors race for. The tight hairpin turns make a course more technical in nature, which requires skill and adds an increased adrenaline rush for the riders.

Chrissy had a major decision to make, and she was pressed for time. She thought to herself, "Would getting dropped from the field shatter my confidence? Should I go to the race for the learning experience? Should I *stick to my guns* and tell Linda that I have already done my last race of the season?" Chrissy knew that she had not done any high-intensity work for over a month, but she wondered if she could still pull off a decent race. Chrissy was in dire need of another perspective to help her make this decision, so she walked into Dr. Landon's office.

Put yourself in Dr. Landon's shoes. What would you say to Chrissy?

Question Guide

1. Describe the characters in this case.
   A. Chrissy
   B. Chrissy's family
   C. Dr. Tucker Landon
   D. Linda Jackson
2. Describe the main issues in this case, and prioritize them.
3. As a sport psychology consultant, generate some courses of action that might help Chrissy.
4. How feasible is each course of action?
5. What are the ramifications of each suggestion?
6. How did Chrissy's attitude and resulting training regime at the beginning of her cycling career set her up for burnout?
7. Has her attitude changed since she has been in graduate school? How?
8. Do you think Chrissy should race at the National Pro Criterium Championship? What are the pros and cons of her competing in this race?

14

ADHERENCE

Rotella's Insights and Observations

One of the qualities that separates successful athletes from the others is the ability to see clearly where they want to go, decide on a process of getting there that they will stick to for a sustained period, and then honor their plan on a day-to-day basis. They stay with it through thick and thin, good times and bad times, when they feel like it and when they don't. Many athletes who don't reach their dreams give up on their process before they get the desired results.

Wimpy Weight Lifter

Shannon D. Reece

"Yo, Matt!" Darryl hollered. "How do you expect to ever compete against the top power lifters if you waste your time on those wimpy circuits?"

"Give it a rest, man. I told you yesterday that the PT's making me do it. She says it's the only way to prevent the pain," Matt threw back, irritated that Darryl was at it again.

"Yeah, like that lady PT has any idea what she's talking about. It's typical: Give a chick a fancy degree, and she thinks she knows everything. You ain't gonna make it unless you learn to push through the pain. Of course, if you can't handle it like a man, there's always the aerobics class at five."

Darryl's last remark stung, as did the laughter from the other guys lifting nearby. They had been unable, and unwilling, to miss the heated exchange. Irritated and uncomfortable with being the center of attention, Matt headed to the other side of the gym. Feeling the need to prove himself, he abandoned his prescribed strengthening circuit and reverted to his old routine, with blatant disregard for the damage he would do to his shoulders.

By the age of 30, Matt had hoped to be ranked in the top five nationally and in the top 15 worldwide among power lifters. Plagued by a recurring shoulder injury, he had begun to fear that his dream would not become a reality. He had less than two years before his 30th birthday. Most lifters reach the peak of their performance by their late twenties to early thirties, and Matt was determined to do the same. Now, however, the pain in his shoulders was taking its toll on his practice schedule. Ridicule, rather than support, was all that he could expect from the other lifters if he continued to give less than 100 percent.

Matt had been introduced to power lifting five years ago by some buddies at the gym. Weight training had been a hobby of his since he finished college. At 5'7" and 260 pounds, he saw himself as short and fat. His receding hairline only added to his own list of personal flaws. As far as academics were concerned, Matt was not particularly strong in any one area. He needed affirmation from the people around him to combat his poor self-image. All the guys were doing it, and he wanted to look good and to fit in.

Matt immediately exhibited signs of natural talent as he progressed rapidly through heavier and heavier lifts without losing his good form. He also quickly gained noticeable muscle definition. A number of trainers at the gym encouraged Matt to pursue power lifting competitively.

Matt experienced early success at local and state competitions in his weight class. As a result, he won the respect he sought from those around him, boosting his self-esteem. His life outside the gym gradually became less important as his emotional attachment to the opinions of other lifters grew stronger. Power lifting success and peer acceptance became the two things on which Matt based his self-worth.

Three months ago, Matt was forced to visit an orthopedic surgeon when the pain in his shoulders had become excruciating. He was diagnosed with bilateral shoulder tendinitis and was referred to a physical therapist named Lisa for treatment. Lisa explained that his overdeveloped chest and middle-back muscles were leading to anterior displacement of the shoulder joints. She prescribed an upper-back routine to counteract the pull his muscles were causing.

Lisa is a brilliant young physical therapist who runs her own practice. She graduated at the top of her class at Ivy University and since then has rehabilitated many elite amateur and professional athletes. She is highly recommended by the sports medicine physicians in the area.

During Lisa's instruction of the new exercises, Matt started complaining that they were "too wimpy." Lisa explained in depth the importance of starting out slow and the need to strengthen his relatively weak upper back muscles to correct the problem. By this time, however, Matt had already begun to doubt her advice. Lisa was up against the "macho mind-set" instilled by many muscle magazines, which often provide false information and damaging training techniques.

Initially, Matt returned to the gym and attempted to follow Lisa's instructions. He was willing to do the exercises as long as no one made fun of him. At first, the comments were mild and came from the less experienced lifters. Then the talented lifters, whom Matt admired, began to make negative comments about his new program and questioned Matt's commitment. Matt's adherence to the rehab ended abruptly. The pain was still present, so he tried resting his shoulders for a few days and then resumed his normal, "nonwimpy" workout schedule. This caused the shoulder tissue to become inflamed again, prompting his return to Lisa to get his shoulders "loosened up."

After four weeks of Matt's resting and then reinjuring his shoulders, Lisa had a serious talk with him. She first tried to get through to him by explaining the futility of his visits and the money he was wasting. When she realized he was still refusing to listen to her, she went a step farther.

"There is no benefit to my loosening your shoulders if you refuse to do the exercises to hold the position," Lisa told him, frustrated that he still wasn't listening.

"You just don't understand that I need to continue to get stronger, and it's a waste of time to do so many reps with hardly any weight," Matt replied. "Can't you just give me some aspirin or something to ease the pain a little?"

"When are you going to learn to listen to your body? It's telling you that something is out of balance. We can set up some goals together for the next couple of weeks, and I promise that you'll see a great reduction in the pain you're experiencing. If you don't start to believe in the rehabilitation, you won't get the results you want. You have a dream to be ranked nationally and worldwide—I understand how important this is to you. I just need you to trust that I know what's best for you right now and that I'm trying to help you achieve your dream by taking care of this injury," Lisa finished, practically pleading with Matt.

Lisa set up some goals, with Matt's input, for the following two weeks. These goals were designed to help him feel some sense of accomplishment and improvement each day. "Follow the exercise schedule we've set up for the next two weeks, and then call me to let me know how your shoulders are feeling. Okay?" Lisa looked up at Matt, anxiously awaiting his response.

"I'll try, but I still think those baby exercises are dumb," Matt fired back.

Two weeks passed, and Lisa did not hear from Matt. At the end of the third week, she called to check on his progress. He said that he had tried to do the exercises at home for a week. When his shoulders began to feel a little better, he returned to the gym, convinced he could resume his regular workouts. It was only a few days before the pain resurfaced.

"I'm so frustrated! I make a little progress, and then I screw it all up because I do what the other guys tell me," Matt said. "I trust them because they've reached the level I want to achieve, and yet their way is not working for me. It's hopeless at this point. I'm never going to reach my dream. I don't even want to go to the gym anymore. At the same time, I feel so empty if I don't go to the gym."

Anxious to offer Matt some hope without pushing him, Lisa paused for a moment and thought about what she wanted to say. After switching the phone to her other ear, she began.

"Matt, I'd like to suggest that you talk with a friend of mine who helps people achieve their performance goals. He's a great guy and is really into lifting in his free time. I think he'll be able to relate to what you're going through and offer some suggestions. How does that sound?" Lisa patiently waited for Matt's response.

"Well, I guess it's worth a shot. At this point I feel that I have nothing to lose." Matt's reply was slow and measured, as his words trailed off.

Lisa gave Matt the name of her friend, Andrew Benton, a sport psychology consultant. Matt made an appointment to meet with Andy two days later at his office. It was apparent to Andy that Matt saw no benefit to this meeting. This attitude was clear from the look of doubt on Matt's face from the moment he walked through the door.

"Matt, why don't you start by telling me what's been happening with your workouts," Andy began. He wanted to allow Matt to lay all the cards out on the table.

"It's just gotten so hard lately. I thought I had found the one thing that I could be really good at, and now it's all falling apart. I really don't know why Lisa wanted me to talk to you. My weight lifting career is over, and I just need to face the fact that I'm going to be a loser for the rest of my life." With that, Matt started to leave with a look of defeat written all over his face.

"Wait a minute, Matt," Andy said. "Why don't you hang out for a while, and we'll talk about this. My time is yours for as long as you need it." Matt returned to his seat with a sigh, as he decided he had nothing better to do with his time at the moment.

If you were Andrew, how would you attempt to help Matt?

Question Guide

1. Describe the characters in this case.
   A. Matt
   B. Darryl
   C. Lisa
   D. Andy Benton
2. Describe the main issues in this case, and prioritize them.
3. What are the factors contributing to Matt's lack of adherence?
4. As a sport psychology consultant, generate some courses of action that might help Matt.
5. How feasible is each course of action?
6. What are the ramifications for Matt of each suggestion?
7. What role does Matt's sense of self-worth play in this situation?
8. What can Andrew do to encourage Matt to adhere to the rehabilitation program assigned by the physical therapist?

The Pressure of the Pull

Shannon D. Reece

THERE WERE ONLY FIVE WEEKS remaining before the Regional Championships (the first qualifying competition) when I got the message. The mother of a young, very talented figure skater named Lexi had called requesting my help. Lexi's mom was concerned about her daughter's mental readiness and wanted someone to assist her in getting some things sorted out before the competition. During my initial phone conversation with Lexi and her mother, I was able to get a feel for the girl's current situation.

"A friend at another rink told me that you really helped him sort some stuff out," Lexi said. "So my mom and I figured you might be able to help me, too."

"Why don't you start by telling me what the problem is," I suggested.

"I feel like I'm a rubber band that is totally stretched out. My coach and our trainer have one end, and my mom and Audrey, the physical therapist, have the other. I'm getting yanked from side to side, which is totally freaking me out. I'm afraid that I'm going to bomb at the Regional Championships." Lexi proceeded to describe how stressful her training environment had become, and her words became punctuated by weak but audible sobs.

"Hey, hey, it's going to be okay, Lexi," I said. "Put your mom on the phone, and we'll set up a time when you, your mom and I can meet. Don't worry, we'll have you ready to knock the socks off those judges in five weeks."

Lexi was able to meet with me over the weekend, following her Saturday practice.

Lexi, a 12-year-old Novice Lady, was a little ball of fire on the ice. She had started taking lessons from her coach, Karen (a former competitive figure skater), at the age of five and had been with her ever since. Karen had a reputation as a very driven, overbearing, and disciplined coach whose control over the lives of her athletes was taken to the extreme. Karen believed in home schooling and off-ice training in ballet, weight lifting, and jazz dance. Whenever possible, Karen had her athletes live with her. If one athlete did not follow her regimen, then none of her athletes would be coached until the athlete (or his or her parents) conformed. Her control extended to the wallets of the parents, as well. Karen's agreement was that no parent would ever receive a bill from her unless an athlete tried to change coaches.

Everything had been fine until Lexi suffered an injury four months ago. She was diagnosed by her physician with a torn hamstring. The doctor told her to stop skating for a couple of weeks to allow the tear to heal. Unfortunately, the rest wasn't enough. When Lexi resumed her training, she immediately reinjured the muscle. Her doctor referred her to Audrey, a well-known physical therapist, for additional treatment.

Audrey began working with Lexi three times a week and revised her training schedule to allow the injury some time to heal. Lexi was to eliminate all stretching, ballet, on-ice jumping, and weight training with Janice, her trainer. To maintain her endurance, Audrey had Lexi ride an exercise bike in place of running. Lexi followed the revised training schedule and treatment with her mom's complete support.

Karen, on the other hand, was considerably upset with the changes in her athlete's practice schedule. She insisted that Lexi continue with her ballet classes if she wanted to maintain her coaching services. Lexi and her mom trusted Audrey's advice and decided to follow the revised training program.

After two weeks, Karen approached Lexi's mom in the lobby of the rink. "This treatment is nonsense," she told her. "All skaters need to stretch. The ballet will keep her muscles loose. I insist that she join the ballet classes again, or I will refuse to train her."

"Karen, you're being completely unreasonable!" Lexi's mom said. "Audrey doesn't want Lexi's hamstring to receive any type of strenuous pull until it has had a chance to heal. I believe she knows what she's doing. She has been very successful in helping a lot of other athletes. I trust that she's doing what's necessary for Lexi to heal."

"I know what's best for my skaters, and I don't need someone like Audrey trying to ruin all I've done to make Lexi the skater she is today! Since I'm not getting any support or cooperation from you or your daughter, I'll take this up with Audrey. I feel like I'm the only one concerned about Lexi's future." Karen's anger was visible as she stormed back toward the rink, muttering under her breath. Lexi's mom was not the type to back down. When it came to Lexi's well-being, she was extremely protective. Though Lexi loved figure skating with a passion, her mom was the driving force behind Lexi's success.

The following week, Karen called Audrey to discuss the situation. Karen was pleasant on the phone, and Audrey was more than happy to provide her with information about Lexi's progress. Audrey explained her reasoning behind the prescribed treatment. While Karen questioned every aspect of the rehab, Audrey remained very patient.

"I'm very concerned about Lexi's endurance," Karen said.

"As I explained, by riding the bike she can maintain her endurance without the impact from running," the therapist replied.

"Well, for her to continue even limited skating would be ridiculous when you don't even want her returning to ballet," the coach stated emphatically. "It's just too much for her leg."

"Actually, I have recommended that she ice-dance," Audrey said. "This type of exercise will strengthen the muscle as it heals without pulling it or causing unnecessary torque."

"Fine. If she needs strengthening, then she can return to Janice for weight training," Karen insisted.

"I don't recommend that at this time. It would be too much too soon. I need you to trust me and allow Lexi to continue her rehabilitation here."

Karen became defensive as she realized she wasn't going to easily regain control over Lexi's life. Audrey, in an attempt to calm her, explained that she wasn't a threat but was only trying to do her job.

As the weeks passed, Karen became more critical and emotional, frustrated by her lack of control over Lexi. The young skater couldn't help but feel the pressure and anger from her coach's feedback. Karen made a point of telling Lexi each day how this change in her training was destroying all the progress they had made and would ultimately result in a very poor showing at the Regional Championships. Lexi trusted Audrey completely and wanted her leg to be 100 percent for the competition as much as her coach did. Karen, however, tried to make Lexi feel guilty and disloyal at every turn.

"I've given you so much of my time and energy," Karen said, "and this is the thanks I get?! I could have been spending my time with a skater who wants to win. You won't have a chance against the other competitors unless you allow me to guide your training. Just stop wasting my valuable time!"

Lexi was in tears by the time Karen finished her angry lecture. Although Lexi was healing physically, she was deteriorating emotionally.

Karen still fought to regain control of her athlete's training. On a number of occasions, she suggested her own form of rehabilitation. Karen finally agreed not to push ballet class until after the Regional Championships. The North Lakes Classic, a state competition, was four weeks away. Lexi and her mom decided that North Lakes would be a dress rehearsal for the Regional Championships.

After Lexi completed her eighth week of rehab, Audrey gave her permission to begin working on her double axel again. Karen was outraged when she learned that Lexi was not given clearance to perform any flexibility moves—spirals, camel spins. She showed her displeasure by refusing to work with Lexi on her double axels. In fact, Karen wasn't coaching Lexi on much of anything.

During the week leading up to the North Lakes Classic, Lexi and her mom decided she should only skate her long program. They agreed that to skate the short program as well might cause too much strain on her leg. They wanted to play it safe with the Regional Championships just over a month away. When Lexi's mom informed Karen of their decision, Karen pulled Lexi from the competition.

"If you won't compete in both events, then you won't compete at all!" Karen stated firmly.

Lexi was devastated by her coach's attitude and began to believe some of the comments she had been making. If Karen thought she was going to do so poorly at the Regional Championships, why should she even try? Karen had been venting all her frustrations on Lexi in the form of constant criticism for many weeks. Physically, Lexi could be ready to compete, but she was becoming a mental basket case with all the tension around her.

With just three days before the North Lake Classic, Lexi's mom calls you and explains the entire story. She sets up an appointment so she and Lexi can meet with you the next day. Right now, they're walking into your office.

Question Guide

1. Describe the characters in this case.
   A. Lexi
   B. Lexi's mom
   C. Karen, the coach
   D. Janice, the weight trainer
   E. Audrey, the physical therapist
2. Describe the main issues in this case, and prioritize them.
3. What are the factors contributing to Lexi's emotional state?
4. As a sport psychology consultant, generate some courses of action that might help Lexi and her mother.
5. How feasible is each course of action?
6. What are the ramifications of each suggestion?
7. What are the responsibilities of the following:
   A. The coach
   B. The trainer
   C. The physical therapist
   D. The sport psychology consultant
8. Should the sport psychology consultant involve the coach and trainer in the session with Lexi? Why or why not?
9. What types of considerations must be taken into account based on the age of the athlete?

15

MOTIVATION

Rotella's Insights
and Observations

It is easier to be motivated when one is new to a sport and regularly sees progress and improvement. Staying motivated is more of a challenge because there is less room for progress and plateaus last longer. But the desire to excel allows successful athletes to look inside themselves and find new ways and reasons to sustain motivation until breakthroughs occur. This skill of self-motivation is greatly influenced by being able to see the desired result in one's mind, and having it serve as the powerful justification for sustaining enthusiasm and persistence.

A Real Pain in the Back

Thomas G. Benoit

"S o, can you go?" Yurri turned away from his best friend, trying not to look because he knew the answer that was coming.

"Of course. The team needs the points. It's only pain." Jalal did not need to hesitate in uttering these words. He had practiced them long before Friday, and he believed them all along.

"It's been quite a trip, hasn't it?" Yurri smiled. He and Jalal began their friendship on a dry August day nearly four years before, at the first Saturday practice for the high school cross-country team.

"Same trip, different roads," Jalal quipped. Both boys smiled. In truth, though, the statement couldn't have been more accurate. Although they quickly became and steadfastly remained each other's "best man," their running talents and successes couldn't have been more dissimilar.

As 14-year-old high school freshmen, Jalal and Yurri began their competitive running days together. At the time, they were both new to distance running. They shared inexperience and slow times. They also shared a newfound belief that commitment and overtraining could make them strong competitors. At the completion of that fall season, they formed a shared goal that they would not lose sight of in the next three years.

As they watched their varsity team fall four team points short of qualifying for the state cross-country meet, they saw a sight that would be burned into their memories. The three seniors on the team, after learning of their failure to advance, huddled together and shed silent tears. Jalal and Yurri vowed that moment that working hard for four years would not go unrewarded, and together they would ensure that no similar fate greeted them at their senior sectionals. As seniors, they would shed no tears together. Even though this goal, this desire, and their friendship would undergo no changes, what each boy could achieve would be most different.

The first spring track season began to draw out the differences in what each boy could accomplish on his own. Running exclusively in junior varsity meets, Yurri

179

quickly found a niche as the top freshman 800-meter runner and distance relay anchor leg. Jalal, slowed by injury, competed when possible and fell toward the back of the freshman and sophomore pack. During the ensuing summer months, the boys trained together when they could, encouraging each other and trying to make good on their goal. Several road races demonstrated that the distance between the two was growing, but both Jalal and Yurri felt that Yurri's success would only mean more benefit for the varsity team and a more solid foundation to what would be their senior cross-country season. They talked about the next three years often and used the talk to push each other to harder and harder workouts.

Unfortunately, the completion of the following fall season was again premature. Yurri and Jalal watched another group of despondent seniors lament an unfulfilled four years. Yurri felt unimportant as the varsity team's seventh runner in the sectional meet; Jalal could only watch as his best friend could not contribute to a top five team finish and a trip to the state meet. Both again promised each other that their senior season would not end as early.

During his sophomore track season, Yurri continued to show marked improvement. He became a varsity regular in the 4 × 800 relay, and it was apparent that his contributions to the team were increasing. Jalal did not enjoy quite the same success, however, despite some improvement in his times. He seemed to be developing much more slowly as a runner, and his significance to the team came in the ranks of the junior varsity distance corps, a group of runners who seemed to be there mostly because they fit nowhere else. The track season seemed to drag on for Jalal, and only talks with Yurri about what they wanted to accomplish as a team could boost his spirits.

The summer provided a much needed change of focus because the world of track could be dropped for the more enjoyable experience of cross-country. The summer allowed the boys time to run together daily, to serve as beacons of focus for each other, and to keep their ultimate purpose alive. They adopted a theory of "always one more mile to run," meaning that whatever they could do in a workout would not be enough. There could always be more. It was this "more" that would make their dream of going to state a reality.

A year passed, and Yurri and Jalal's junior season held both encouraging improvements and unthinkable disaster. Yurri established himself as a top four runner on the team and a primary point scorer in all meets and invitationals. Jalal overcame time barriers that had seemed to haunt him all summer and early fall. He was finally on the verge of breaking into the varsity seven, the group that would run and score in all meets. However, the season ended in bitter disappointment, as the team, which had narrowly missed states for two successive years, faltered in regionals and didn't give itself a chance in the sectional. Jalal and Yurri watched in horror as the team they were trying to build for the upcoming year seemed to take a giant step in the wrong direction. The morning following the regional disaster, Jalal and Yurri met for breakfast and laid out the plans that they thought would deliver their goals in the next 12 months.

The ensuing spring track season saw glimmers of hope for both boys. Yurri steadily improved in the 800. With him running third leg on the 4 × 800 relay with the other top cross-country runners, the relay team qualified for the state track finals. Jalal continued to train with the distance corps but also added regular attempts at other events in order to find a way to contribute to the varsity team. By becoming an "event vagrant," Jalal could find himself in almost any event if injury to a regular occurred or if an unfatigued body was needed in a meet where he could actually score points. Although Jalal enjoyed the season much more than the previous two track campaigns, he realized that his net contributions to the varsity score sheet were minimal.

Unquestionably, however, the greatest accomplishment of both runners during the spring was the recruitment of the following fall's cross-country team. In the past three years, the boys' team had never exceeded 16 runners. Through much persuasion and the offering of a state meet appearance, Jalal and Yurri lured a total of 24 runners to help them achieve their goal. The notion of what could happen also fueled the most intense off-season training the two boys had known, particularly for Jalal. Wanting the best for the team, but also wanting desperately to contribute, Jalal knew he would have to improve to be in the varsity seven and to see his goal come to fruition.

The fall season began impressively for the boys and the team. Yurri was a solid number three runner, and Jalal was in the seventh position. The early season saw numerous team successes, and the individual talent continued to grow. As the season neared the halfway mark, Jalal was challenged by three of the runners he and Yurri had recruited for the seventh and final varsity position. Jalal, wanting to contribute to the team's success and help the team reach the state meet, began daily 6:00 A.M. runs of seven miles. By late in the season, though, Jalal lost his position. Overtrained and fatigued, he faded to the number nine slot. His cross-county season ended before the postseason even began. His four years of work to contribute to his team came and went, and he was only able to watch as Yurri and the other six varsity runners advanced to state and placed tenth as a team. Jalal felt completely insignificant.

During the winter of his senior year, Jalal became extremely motivated. He had watched his cross-country dreams go by in someone else's shoes. He had only one more season to be a significant contributor, and he could not lose that as well. Yurri saw all this, and all winter long placed his final track goals next to Jalal's. Together, they would lift and run and try to find some way to share their last competitive season together. Yurri's role was already defined as an 800-meter runner and 4 × 800 relay leg. He had helped set a school record the previous spring and was aiming for a state medal this time around. Jalal would again fill the "event vagrant" role, always looking for the chance to compete and contribute. Fortunately, he also filled a regular role. As the track team had no returning pole vaulters, Jalal took up this event with great zeal. Although he could not, in one year, master his new event, he did become skilled enough to score points in the smaller meets and invitationals. As the season continued, everyone felt not only that Jalal had recovered from his overtrained condition, but that he would also be a major contributor in one of the year's biggest meets.

When the track sectionals were outlined for the team, the chance for the track team's first sectional title seemed realistic. The competition looked to be very tight between three schools, with every point being highly contested. For Jalal, this news generated personal excitement, as he knew his section was devoid of vaulters. With only five entered in the section, clearing any height would guarantee points for his team. Defeating one or two other vaulters would enhance his team's chance of winning the title. It was with this excitement that Jalal entered the final regular season meet, six days before the sectional. It was with this excitement that disaster struck on his first vault of the regular meet.

On his first attempt at an opening height of ten feet, Jalal barreled down the runway, planted his pole, and soared toward the bar. At the crest of his arc, he tucked his legs around the bar, threw his torso back, and brushed the bar with his chest on the way down. Watching the bar shake as he dropped toward the pits, Jalal was jolted by pain emanating from his lower back. He had dropped just in front of the pits and landed square in the metal plant box from where his pole had sent him skyward. The pain was searing.

At the hospital, X rays revealed a fracture of his second lumbar vertebra. Jalal could see the fracture line himself; he could feel the spasm in his lower back. This did not stop him from convincing himself that he would be fine in six days. He asked the emergency room physician about returning to vaulting. The physician greeted the question with an uncertain grin and referred him to an orthopedic specialist. The specialist told Jalal that he could vault without risking much more damage if he could deal with the pain. Jalal assured the specialist he could. However, Jalal's family physician couldn't understand why he'd want to and advised against all strenuous activity for three weeks. Jalal's parents asked him not to vault. His teammates encouraged him to try, and his coach left the decision up to him.

He had yet to touch a pole since the previous Saturday. He hadn't even tried jogging, let alone sprinting. He sat down next to Yurri at lunch on Wednesday. Yurri glanced at his "best man" and asked, "So, can you go?"

As lunch ended, Jalal found himself less sure about vaulting. He decides to think this through with someone who understood and could help.

Now he's walking into your office.

Question Guide

1. Describe the characters in this case.
   A. Jalal
   B. Yurri
   C. Their track teammates
   D. The orthopedic specialist
2. Describe the main issues in this case, and prioritize them.
3. How will the friendship between Jalal and Yurri affect the former's decision about vaulting in the upcoming meet?
4. As a sport psychology consultant, generate some courses of action that might help Jalal.
5. How feasible is each course of action?
6. What are the ramifications of each suggestion?
7. What are the responsibilities of the coach? Did the coach fulfill his responsibility?
8. Should the sport psychology consultant involve the coach or Yurri in the session with Jalal? Why or why not?
9. Is the risk of further injury worth taking?
10. If you had been working with this team as a sport psychology consultant for several months prior to the sectional meet, what would you have worked on with the team? With Jalal?

Way Too Early

Bill Allyson

I'VE ALWAYS ENJOYED WATCHING high school and college wrestling, even though I was in my basketball season every year when the wrestlers were competing. It was probably because we shared a locker room in high school and I got to be good friends with many of the better wrestlers on our team. After entering graduate school in sport psychology, I asked the wrestling coach if I could come to practices and help out wherever he needed me. He had no problem with that, and I've been coming two or three times a week.

I've gotten to know many of the better wrestlers on the team here at the University of Banff, mostly because they take the time to come over and ask how I'm doing. Three weeks ago, Coach Hurley and I talked for over two hours in his office, and he asked me to talk to the team for about 20 minutes before practice. I did that, and I've spoken with them twice more, once each week. During the last three weeks, the younger wrestlers have also been making casual conversation with me at practice and around the athletic complex. As I sat there today, it felt good that I've fit in so well with the guys on this team in such a short time.

Just as I was thinking that, one of the young wrestlers came up to me. "Excuse me," he began, "Coach said I could take time out of practice to talk to you. Is there somewhere we could go and talk privately?"

We walked upstairs to an empty conference room, talking generally about wrestling and the successful tradition of the Banff program. Once in the room we closed the door and sat down. Extending my hand I said, "I'm Breht, but I don't believe I know your name."

"I'm Julio, but the guys call me Scrappy. I just wanted to talk with you because I've been having trouble with the morning workouts. You see, I don't have any problem getting up at 5:45 A.M. like a lot of the other guys do. For me it's just that I don't feel like being at wrestling at that hour of the morning. In fact, I've been beginning to think that I don't feel like being at wrestling practice any time lately."

Julio paused to look me squarely in the eye. It seemed like he had much more to say, so I asked him, "What more can you tell me about this?"

"Well, I'm a redshirt freshman this year, so I don't get to wrestle in any meets for the school until next fall. But I get to practice against Bart, the number two guy in the nation, almost every day, and that should be exciting to me. He'll graduate after this year, and it's between me and Sam to move into the starting spot at 177 pounds.

"You know, when you got us to discuss our roles and responsibilities as members of the team last week, it made all the sense in the world that wrestling against the number two guy was some of the best practice I could possibly get. That in itself was exciting to other guys on the team who wrestle against ranked guys. But I just don't get excited about wrestling the number two guy, or anybody else, these days. And none of the other excitement or fun the other guys talked about in our meeting has worked for me either. I just come here and go through the motions.

"I didn't used to be that way. When I was in high school, I would bug coach to come back at night and let me and a couple other guys onto the mats so I could get an extra workout against them. And they weren't ranked or anything, but I just wanted to wrestle more. That's how I learned my single leg, double leg, and high crotch moves. Those moves had a lot to do with me being a three-time state champion, which in turn got me a scholarship here. Yet now that I've been here six months or so, I almost couldn't care less about a single leg or a high crotch takedown. I've seen that feeling fizzle away to almost nothing.

"Take last Wednesday morning, for example. The coaches told us who we were going to wrestle the night before, and they also said we'd be working on the high crotch, my best move. I can hit that move even against Bart, which tells me I can likely do it against anyone in the country. But I came in that morning not feeling any particular excitement about what we were about to do, and it showed in my performance. I didn't hit one solid high crotch that Bart didn't give me. And I didn't care! I realized, during practice, that I was way out of it and basically said 'So what' to myself. That's not like me, at least the me that wrestled well the last three years.

"So I'd like to know, from you, what you think I can do to be more excited about morning practice and practice in general. It's gotten to the point where I would just as soon not wrestle anymore than come in here and give a half-baked effort."

Question Guide

1. Describe the characters in this case.
   A. Breht, the sport psychology consultant
   B. Coach Hurley
   C. Julio
   D. Julio's teammates
2. Describe the main issues in this case, and prioritize them.
3. What factors contribute to Julio's lack of performance on the mats?
4. As a sport psychology consultant, generate some courses of action that might help Julio.
5. How feasible is each course of action?
6. What are the ramifications of each suggestion?
7. Are there any deeper issues that a sport psychology consultant should consider?
8. Would you involve the coach in the sessions with Julio? Why or why not?

Appendices

Teaching Suggestions

Introduction

The preparation and actual teaching of a case are just as time-consuming as that of a lecture, especially if this approach is new to the instructor. Instructors must be prepared for the discussion to stray off course and to bring the group back on course. However, many times the "sidetrack" discussions prove just as fruitful as the intended discussion. Therefore, the instructor must be prepared to deal with both the planned sequence of events as well as the unplanned discussions.

As an instructor, your enthusiasm is a vital element in the case-study teaching approach. If you are unsure and apprehensive about the case-study process, the resulting case discussion may be less than ideal. You must accept the possibility that the case may not go perfectly the first time through. As with any other teaching method, practice is needed.

Organizational Considerations

One method for emphasizing and organizing important points is the prudent use of a chalkboard or large paper tablet. By recording comments in front of the class, you help the group focus on the main points. It also serves as a reminder to the students that they are contributing to the discussion.

The arrangement of the classroom furniture can either facilitate or inhibit the class discussion. Desks or tables should be placed in a U shape so that all participants can see one another, you, and the chalkboard or tablet.

Portions of this section, reprinted with permission from the *Journal of Physical Education, Recreation & Dance*, appeared in Boyce, B. A., *Making the Case for the Case-Method Approach in Physical Education Pedagogy Classes*, August, 1992, pages 17–20. JOPERD is a publication of the American Alliance for Health, Physical Education, Recreation and Dance, 1990 Association Dr., Reston, VA 22091.

CASE STUDIES IN SPORT PSYCHOLOGY

Class Participation

Using volunteers to answer questions is probably better than calling on students because it enhances group discussion and it differs from the recitation of facts and theory that often accompanies a lecture-style class. However, as the instructor, you must be aware of students who dominate the discussion. One way to include everyone is to practice "wait time." Many students will speak up if you allow them time to collect and present their thoughts. Allowing students wait time may also improve the quality of their responses.

When teaching a case, be careful not to express your opinion on possible alternatives to solve the dilemma. Students are always interested in how the instructor or an experienced sport psychology consultant might have handled the particular situation. Even though it would be easy and ego-satisfying to furnish students with your solutions, this action may have a detrimental effect on the future discussion of cases. After all, the goal of the case-study approach is to involve students in the generation and evaluation of alternatives.

Time Considerations

Keeping track of the time is difficult in this type of teaching approach. Most instructors must use a clock, and many instructors impose a time limit for the beginning, middle, and final segments of each case. Bringing closure to the discussion is critical if the case will not be covered again in the next class and you wish to end the discussion. However, if you want the issues or points to continue in the next class, it might be best not to summarize.

When to Use the Case-Study Approach

The case-study approach must be integrated into the existing curriculum. The strength of the case-study approach is that it encourages students to generate solutions to issues or problems that are not easily discernible and are multifaceted (e.g., anxiety, team cohesion, confidence).

Cases can be offered as a culminating experience in a unit (e.g., aggression in sport). The information obtained through this exercise could serve to inform the instructor about how well the students grasped the concepts and about their ability to apply these concepts. In contrast, the case could also serve as an introductory exercise for students to express their views regarding a construct in sport psychology. The second approach might be used if students are at the graduate level and already possess both experience in the sport environment and mastery of the literature and research in the area addressed by the case. The case-study approach offers a safe means of developing skills for consulting with coaches and athletes, especially if you are willing to include role-playing as a part of the case discussion.

Breaking the class up into small groups (three per group is ideal) will allow students to role-play. In groups of three, one student can comment while or after the others role-play. In this way, question guides become flexible, adjusting for the responses given. You might require question guides early in the course, but as the students gain experience, ask them to role-play "cold" or without reading the case or relying on the question guide.

Question Guide

The list of questions that accompanies each case should function as a guide. When reading through the cases, it becomes evident that each case has a main theme, but there are also many subthemes that can emerge as a part of the class discussion. As the instructor, you will need to decide when a discussion is pertinent to the topic under deliberation or when the group has strayed. You may want to create or add to an existing question guide before using a case in class. You can refocus the class by restating questions from the question guide. However, you should not act hastily to refocus the discussion away from a subtheme; this type of discussion might produce valuable insights to other aspects of the case. It is your call.

One strategy in case-study teaching involves restating or reworking the question guide to account for the alternative foci of discussion. This can be done immediately following the case discussion, using a reflective process, or while the discussion is in progress. A combination of processes (reflection after the completion of the case and during the case) is suggested.

Suggested References

The Suggested References provided in this book can be used to substantiate the approaches taken by the students to resolve the issues in each case. Since this list of references could not possibly be complete, you may wish to use one of the following alternatives to enhance this aspect of the learning experience. First, you could provide students with additional references for each topic. Clearly, more references exist, some of which may be of significance to you or to the focus of the class. Second, you could have the students provide additional references, along with their rationales for choosing those materials. These alternatives foster greater familiarity with the most useful literature and enhance the independence of your students.

Suggested References

In formulating your response to each case, you will apply sport psychology theory. The following list provides recommended references (of the many available) for theory and application relevant to the topics and the cases presented in this book.

Interventions in Sport Psychology

Cox, R. H., Qui, Y., & Lui, Z. (1993). Overview of sport psychology. In R. N. Singer, M. Murphey, & L. K. Tennant (Eds.), *Handbook of research on sport psychology* (pp. 3-31). New York: Macmillan.

Danish, S. J., Petitpas, A., & Hale, B. D. (1995). Psychological interventions: A life development model. In S. M. Murphy (Ed.), *Sport psychology interventions*, (pp. 19-38). Champaign, IL: Human Kinetics.

Gill, D. L. (1986). Behavior modification in sport. In D. L. Gill, *Psychological dynamics of sport* (pp. 133-146). Champaign, IL: Human Kinetics.

Kirschenbaum, D. S., & Wittrock, D. A. (1984). Cognitive-behavioral interventions in sport: A self-regulatory perspective. In J. M. Silva & R. S. Weinberg (Eds.), *Psychological foundations of sport* (pp. 81-97). Champaign, IL: Human Kinetics.

Williams, J. M., & Leffingwell, T. R. (1996). Cognitive strategies in sport and exercise psychology. In J. L. Van Raalte & B. W. Brewer (Eds.), *Exploring sport and exercise psychology* (pp. 51-74). Washington, DC: American Psychological Association.

Chapter 1: Anxiety and Arousal

Cox, R. H. (1990). Anxiety in sport. In R. H. Cox, *Sport psychology: Concepts and applications* (pp. 119-142). Dubuque, IA: Wm. C. Brown.

Cox, R. H. (1990). Arousal in sport. In R. H. Cox, *Sport psychology: Concepts and applications* (pp. 87-116). Dubuque, IA: Wm. C. Brown.

Cox, R. H. (1990). Intervention strategies. In R. H. Cox, *Sport psychology: Concepts and applications* (pp. 143-190). Dubuque, IA: Wm. C. Brown.

Gill, D. L. (1986). Arousal and sport performance. In D. L. Gill, *Psycholygical dynamics of sport* (pp. 113-132). Champaign, IL: Human Kinetics.

Gill, D. L. (1986). Competitiveness and competitive anxiety. In D. L. Gill, *Psychological dynamics of sport* (pp. 55-78). Champaign, IL: Human Kinetics.

Gould, D., & Krane, V. (1992). The arousal-athletic performance relationship: Current status and future directions. In T. S. Horn (Ed.), *Advances in sport psychology* (pp. 119-142). Champaign, IL: Human Kinetics.

Hackfort, D., & Schwenkmezger, P. (1993). Anxiety. In R. N. Singer, M. Murphey, & L. K. Tennant (Eds.), *Handbook of research on sport psychology* (pp. 328-364). New York: Macmillan.

Hackfort, D., & Spielberger, C. D. (Eds.). (1984). *Anxiety in sports: An international perspective*. New York: Hemisphere.

Harris, D. V., & Harris, B. L. (1984). Worry and anxiety about performance. In D. V. Harris & B. L. Harris, *The athlete's guide to sport psychology: Mental skills for physical people* (pp. 29-76). Champaign, IL: Leisure Press.

Landers, D. M., & Boutcher, S. H. (1986). Arousal-performance relationships. In J. M. Williams (Ed.), *Applied sport psychology: Personal growth to peak performance* (pp. 163-184). Mountain View, CA: Mayfield.

Roberts, G. C., Spink, K. S., & Pemberton, C. L. (1986). Anxiety. In G. C. Roberts, K. S. Spink, & C. L. Pemberton, *Learning experiences in sport psychology* (pp. 63-70). Champaign, IL: Human Kinetics.

Smith, R. E. (1984). Theoretical and treatment approaches to anxiety reduction. In J. M. Silva & R. S. Weinberg (Eds.), *Psychological foundations of sport* (pp. 157-169). Champaign, IL: Human Kinetics.

Sonstroem, F. J. (1984). An overview of anxiety in sport. In J. M. Silva & R. S. Weinberg (Eds.), *Psychological foundations of sport* (pp. 104-117). Champaign, IL: Human Kinetics.

Weinberg, R. S. (1984). Mental preparation strategies. In J. M. Silva & R. S. Weinberg (Eds.), *Psychological foundations of sport* (pp. 145-156). Champaign, IL: Human Kinetics.

Zaichkowsky, L., & Takenaka, K. (1993). In R. N. Singer, M. Murphey, & L. K. Tennant (Eds.), *Handbook of research on sport psychology* (pp. 511-527). New York: Macmillan.

Chapter 2: Interpersonal Relations

Coppel, D. B. (1995). Relationship issues in sport: A marital therapy model. In S. M. Murphy (Ed.), *Sport psychology interventions* (pp. 193-204.) Champaign, IL: Human Kinetics.

Gardner, F. (1995). The coach and the team psychologist: An integrated organizational model. In S. M. Murphy (Ed.), *Sport psychology interventions* (pp. 147-176). Champaign, IL: Human Kinetics.

Gill, D. L. (1986). Interpersonal relationships in sport groups. In D. L. Gill, *Psychological dynamics of sport* (pp. 221-234). Champaign, IL: Human Kinetics.

Hanrahan, S., & Gallois, C. (1993). In R. N. Singer, M. Murphey, & L. K. Tennant (Eds.), *Handbook of research on sport psychology* (pp. 623-646). New York: Macmillan.

Harris, D. V., & Harris, B. L. (1984). Communication: Learning to say what you mean or meaning what you say! In D. V. Harris & B. L. Harris, *The athlete's guide to sport psychology: Mental skills for physical people* (pp. 147-164). Champaign, IL: Leisure Press.

Martens, R. (1987). Communication skills. In R. Martens, *Coaches' guide to sport psychology* (pp. 47-66). Champaign, IL: Human Kinetics.

Orlick, T. (1990). Solving problems with coaches. In T. Orlick, *In pursuit of excellence: How to win in sport and life through mental training* (pp. 133-142). Champaign, IL: Leisure Press.

Chapter 3: Team Cohesion

Carron, A. V. (1984). Cohesion in sport teams. In J. M. Silva & R. S. Weinberg (Eds.), *Psychological foundations of sport* (pp. 340-352). Champaign, IL: Human Kinetics.

Carron, A. V. (1986). The sport team as an effective group. In J. M. Williams (Ed.), *Applied sport psychology: Personal growth to peak performance* (pp. 75-92). Mountain View, CA: Mayfield.

Chelladurai, P. (1984). Leadership in sports. In J. M. Silva & R. S. Weinberg (Eds.), *Psychological foundations of sport* (pp. 329-339). Champaign, IL: Human Kinetics.

Chelladurai, P. (1993). Leadership. In R. N. Singer, M. Murphey, & L. K. Tennant (Eds.), *Handbook of research on sport psychology* (pp. 647-671). New York: Macmillan.

Cox, R. H. (1990). Leadership in sport. In R. H. Cox, *Sport psychology: Concepts and applications* (pp. 371-416). Dubuque, IA: Wm. C. Brown.

Cox, R. H. (1990). Team cohesion. In R. H. Cox, *Sport psychology: Concepts and applications* (pp. 335-370). Dubuque, IA: Wm. C. Brown.

Gill, D. L. (1984). Individual and group performance in sport. In J. M. Silva & R. S. Weinberg (Eds.), *Psychological foundations of sport* (pp. 315-328). Champaign, IL: Human Kinetics.

Gill, D. L. (1986). Individual and group performance in sport. In D. L. Gill, *Psychological dynamics of sport* (pp. 209-220). Champaign, IL: Human Kinetics.

Hanrahan, S., & Gallois, C. (1993). In R. N. Singer, M. Murphey, & L. K. Tennant (Eds.), *Handbook of research on sport psychology* (pp. 623-646). New York: Macmillan.

Orlick, T. (1986). Building team harmony. In T. Orlick, *Psyching for sport: Mental training for athletes* (pp. 95-102). Champaign, IL: Leisure Press.

Orlick, T. (1990). Team harmony. In T. Orlick, *In pursuit of excellence: How to win in sport and life through mental training* (pp. 143-152). Champaign, IL: Leisure Press.

Roberts, G. C., Spink, K. S., & Pemberton, C. L. (1986). Cohesion. In G. C. Roberts, K. S. Spink, & C. L. Pemberton, *Learning experiences in sport psychology* (pp. 93-98). Champaign, IL: Human Kinetics.

Widmeyer, W. N., Brawley, L. R., & Carron, A. V. (1992). Group dynamics in sport. In T. S. Horn (Ed.), *Advances in sport psychology* (pp. 163-180). Champaign, IL: Human Kinetics.

Widmeyer, W. N., Carron, A. V., & Brawley, L. R. (1993). In R. N. Singer, M. Murphey, L. K. Tennant (Eds.), *Handbook of research on sport psychology* (pp. 672-692). New York: Macmillan.

Yukelson, D. P. (1984). Group motivation in sport teams. In J. M. Silva & R. S. Weinberg (Eds.), *Psychological foundations of sport* (pp. 229-240). Champaign, IL: Human Kinetics.

Chapter 4: Aggressiveness and Assertiveness

Cox, R. H. (1990). Aggression in sport. In R. H. Cox, *Sport psychology: Concepts and applications* (pp. 263-302). Dubuque, IA: Wm. C. Brown.

Gill, D. L. (1986). Aggression in sport. In D. L. Gill, *Psychological dynamics of sport* (pp. 193-206). Champaign, IL: Human Kinetics.

Husman, B. F., & Silva, J. M. (1984). Aggression in sport: Definitional and theoretical considerations. In J. M. Silva & R. S. Weinberg (Eds.), *Psychological foundations of sport* (pp. 246-260). Champaign, IL: Human Kinetics.

Roberts, G. C., Spink, K. S., & Pemberton, C. L. (1986). Aggression. In G. C. Roberts, K. S. Spink, & C. L. Pemberton, *Learning experiences in sport psychology* (pp. 71-76). Champaign, IL: Human Kinetics.

Silva, J. M. (1984). Factors related to the acquisition and exhibition of aggressive sport behavior. In J. M. Silva & R. S. Weinberg (Eds.), *Psychological foundations of sport* (pp. 261-273). Champaign, IL: Human Kinetics.

Thirer, J. (1993). Aggression. In R. N. Singer, M. Murphey, & L. K. Tennant (Eds.), *Handbook of research on sport psychology* (pp. 365-378). New York: Macmillan.

Widmeyer, W. N. (1984). Aggression-performance relationships in sport. In J. M. Silva & R. S. Weinberg (Eds.), *Psychological foundations of sport* (pp. 274-285). Champaign, IL: Human Kinetics.

Chapter 5: Confidence

Bunker, L., & Williams, J. M. (1986). Cognitive techniques for improving performance and building confidence. In J. M. Williams (Ed.), *Applied sport psychology: Personal growth to peak performance* (pp. 235-256). Mountain View, CA: Mayfield.

Martens, R. (1987). Self-confidence and goal-setting skills. In R. Martens, *Coaches' guide to sport psychology* (pp. 151-170). Champaign, IL: Human Kinetics.

Orlick, T. (1986). Consistency and confidence. In T. Orlick, *Psyching for sport: Mental training for athletes* (pp. 87-94). Champaign, IL: Leisure Press.

Chapter 6: Expectations of Others

Harris, D. V., & Harris, B. L. (1984). Concentration: Directing your attentional focus. In D. V. Harris & B. L. Harris, *The athlete's guide to sport psychology: Mental skills for physical people* (pp. 77-94). Champaign, IL: Leisure Press.

Horn, T. S. (1986). The self-fulfilling prophecy theory: When coaches' expectations become reality. In J. M. Williams (Ed.), *Applied sport psychology: Personal growth to peak performance* (pp. 59-74). Mountain View, CA: Mayfield.

Orlick, T. (1990). From hero to zero. In T. Orlick, *In pursuit of excellence: How to win in sport and life through mental training* (pp. 167-176). Champaign, IL: Leisure Press.

Roberts, G. C., Spink, K. S., & Pemberton, C. L. (1986). Social facilitation. In G. C. Roberts, K. S. Spink, & C. L. Pemberton, *Learning experiences in sport psychology* (pp. 45-56). Champaign, IL: Human Kinetics.

Wankel, L. (1984). Audience effects in sport. In J. M. Silva & R. S. Weinberg (Eds.), *Psychological foundations of sport* (pp. 188-196). Champaign, IL: Human Kinetics.

Chapter 7: Composure and Emotional Control

Crews, D. J. (1993). Self-regulation strategies in sport and exercise. In R. N. Singer, M. Murphey, & L. K. Tennant (Eds.), *Handbook of research on sport psychology* (pp. 557-568) New York: Macmillan.

Orlick, T. (1990). Gaining control. In T. Orlick, *In pursuit of excellence: How to win in sport and life through mental training* (pp. 49-64). Champaign, IL: Leisure Press.

Taylor, J. (1996). Intensity regulation and athletic performance. In J. L. Van Raalte & B. W. Brewer (Eds.), *Exploring sport and exercise psychology* (pp. 75-106). Washington, DC: American Psychological Association.

Chapter 8: Psychological Rehabilitation

May, J. R., & Sieb, G. E. (1987). Athletic injuries: Psychosocial factors in the onset, sequelae, rehabilitation, and prevention. In J. R. May & M. J. Asken (Eds.), *Sport psychology: The psychological health of the athlete* (pp. 157-186). New York: PMA.

Petitpas, A., & Danish, S. J. (1995). Caring for injured athletes. In S. M. Murphy (Ed.), *Sport psychology interventions*. Champaign, IL: Human Kinetics.

Rotella, R. J., & Heyman, S. R. (1986). Stress, injury, and the psychological rehabilitation of athletes. In J. M. Williams (Ed.), *Applied sport psychology: Personal growth to peak performance* (pp. 343-364). Mountain View, CA: Mayfield.

Charter 9: Dedication and Commitment

Harris, D. V., & Harris, B. L. (1984). Staying on track: Avoiding obstacles. In D. V. Harris & B. L. Harris, *The athlete's guide to sport psychology: Mental skills for physical people* (pp. 165-178). Champaign, IL: Leisure Press.

Henschen, K. P. (1986). Athletic staleness and burnout: Diagnosis, prevention, and treatment. In J. M. Williams (Ed.), *Applied sport psychology: Personal growth to peak performance* (pp. 327-342). Mountain View, CA: Mayfield.

Orlick, T. (1990). Commitment and excellence. In T. Orlick, *In pursuit of excellence: How to win in sport and life through mental training* (pp. 7-14). Champaign, IL: Leisure Press.

Chapter 10: Discipline

Livingston, M. K. (1989). *Mental discipline: The pursuit of peak performance*. Champaign, IL: Human Kinetics.

Chapter 11: Ethics

Sachs, M. (1993). Professional ethics in sport psychology. In R. N. Singer, M. Murphey, & L. K. Tennant (Eds.), *Handbook of research on sport psychology* (pp. 921-932). New York: Macmillan.

Whelan, J. P., Meyers, A. W., & Elkin, T. D. (1996). Ethics in sport and exercise psychology. In J. L. Van Raalte & B. W. Brewer (Eds.), *Exploring sport and exercise psychology* (pp. 431-447). Washington, DC: American Psychological Association.

Chapter 12: Goal Setting and Planning

Burton, D. (1992). The Jekyll/Hyde nature of goals: Reconceptualizing goal setting in sport. In T. S. Horn (Ed.), *Advances in sport psychology* (pp. 267-298). Champaign, IL: Human Kinetics.

Burton, D. (1993). Goal setting in sport. In R. N. Singer, M. Murphey, & L. K. Tennant (Eds.), *Handbook of research on sport psychology* (pp. 467-491). New York: Macmillan.

Duda, J. L. (1993). Goals: A social cognitive approach to the study of achievement motivation in sport. In R. N. Singer, M. Murphey, & L. K. Tennant (Eds.), *Handbook of research on sport psychology* (pp. 421-436). New York: Macmillan.

Gould, D. (1986). Goal setting for peak performance. In J. M. Williams (Ed.), *Applied sport psychology: Personal growth to peak performance* (pp. 133-148). Mountain View, CA: Mayfield.

Harris, D. V., & Harris, B. L. (1984). Goal setting: The regulation of motivation. In D. V. Harris & B. L. Harris, *The athlete's guide to sport psychology: Mental skills for physical people* (pp. 133-146). Champaign, IL: Leisure Press.

O'Block, F. R., & Evans, F. H. (1984). Goal setting as a motivational technique. In J. M. Silva & R. S. Weinberg (Eds.), *Psychological foundations of sport* (pp. 188-196). Champaign, IL: Human Kinetics.

Orlick, T. (1986). Targets and goals. In T. Orlick, *Psyching for sport: Mental training for athletes* (pp. 5-18). Champaign, IL: Leisure Press.

Weinberg, R. S. (1996). Goal setting in sport and exercise: Research to practice. In J. L. Van Raalte & B. W. Brewer (Eds.), *Exploring sport and exercise psychology* (pp. 3-24). Washington, DC: American Psychological Association.

Chapter 13: Attitude

Gill, D. L. (1986). Attitudes and sport behavior. In D. L. Gill, *Psychological dynamics of sport* (pp. 95-110). Champaign, IL: Human Kinetics.

Chapter 14: Adherence

Dishman, R. K. (1984). Motivation and exercise adherence. In J. M. Silva & R. S. Weinberg (Eds.), *Psychological foundations of sport* (pp. 420-434). Champaign, IL: Human Kinetics.

Dishman, R K. (1994). *Advances in exercise adherence*. Champaign, IL; Human Kinetics.

Marcus, B. H., Bock, B. C., Pinto, B. M., & Clark, B. M. (1996). Exercise initiation, adoption, and maintenance. In J. L. Van Raalte & B. W. Brewer (Eds.), *Exploring sport and exercise psychology* (pp. 133-158). Washington, DC: American Psychological Association.

Roberts, G. C., Spink, K. S., & Pemberton, C. L. (1986). Exercise adherence. In G. C. Roberts, K. S. Spink, & C. L. Pemberton, *Learning experience in sport psychology* (pp. 133-138). Champaign, IL: Human Kinetics.

Chapter 15: Motivation

Brawley, L. R., & Roberts, G. C. (1984). Attributions in sport: Research foundations, characteristics, and limitations. In J. M. Silva & R. S. Weinberg (Eds.), *Psychological foundations of sport* (pp. 197-213). Champaign, IL: Human Kinetics.

Cox, R. H. (1990). Achievement motivation. In R. H. Cox, *Sport psychology: Concepts and applications* (pp. 193-224). Dubuque, IA: Wm. C. Brown.

Gill, D. L. (1986). Cognitive approaches: Intrinsic motivation in sport. In D. L. Gill, *Psychological dynamics of sport* (pp. 147-170). Champaign, IL: Human Kinetics.

Harris, D. V., & Harris, B. L. (1984). Goal setting: The regulation of motivation. In D. V. Harris & B. L. Harris, *The athlete's guide to sport psychology: Mental skills for physical people* (pp. 133-146). Champaign, IL: Leisure Press.

Martens, R. (1987). Motivation. In R. Martens, *Coaches' guide to sport psychology* (pp. 15-30) Champaign, IL: Human Kinetics.

O'Block, F. R., & Evans, F. H. (1984). Goal setting as a motivational technique. In J. M. Silva & R. S. Weinberg (Eds.), *Psychological foundations of sport* (pp. 188-196). Champaign, IL: Human Kinetics.

Roberts, G. C. (1984). Toward a new theory of motivation in sport: The role of perceived ability. In J. M. Silva & R. S. Weinberg (Eds.), *Psychological foundations of sport* (pp. 214-228). Champaign, IL: Human Kinetics.

Roberts, G. C. (1992). *Motivation in sport and exercise.* Champaign, IL: Human Kinetics.

Roberts, G. C., Spink, K. S., & Pemberton, C. L. (1986). Motivation. In G. C. Roberts, K. S. Spink, & C. L. Pemberton, *Learning experiences in sport psychology* (pp. 77-92). Champaign, IL: Human Kinetics.

Weinberg, R. S. (1984). The relationship between extrinsic rewards and intrinsic motivation in sport. In J. M. Silva & R. S. Weinberg (Eds.), *Psychological foundations of sport* (pp. 177-187). Champaign, IL: Human Kinetics.

Weiss, M. R., & Chaumeton, N. (1992). Motivational orientations in sport. In T. S. Horn (Ed.), *Advances in sport psychology* (pp. 61-100). Champaign, IL: Human Kinetics.

3656

3656